Spiralize It!

Spiralize It!

A Cookbook of Creative Spiralizer Recipes
for Every Type of Eater

Kenzie Swanhart

Photography by Shannon Douglas

SONOMA
PRESS

For Julien, my best friend and the love of my life.

For general information on our other products and services or to obtain technical support, please contact our Customer Care Department within the United States at (866) 744-2665, or outside the United States at (510) 253-0500.

Sonoma Press publishes its books in a variety of electronic and print formats. Some content that appears in print may not be available in electronic books, and vice versa.

TRADEMARKS: Sonoma Press and the Sonoma Press logo are trademarks or registered trademarks of Arcas Publishing, a Callisto Media Inc. company and/or its affiliates, in the United States and other countries, and may not be used without written permission. All other trademarks are the property of their respective owners. Sonoma Press is not associated with any product or vendor mentioned in this book.

Photography © 2015 by Shannon Douglas
Photo on page 14 courtesy of Brieftons.
http://www.brieftons.com
Author photo © 2015 by Julien Levesque

ISBN: Print 978-1-942411-98-7 | eBook 978-1-942411-99-4

CONTENTS

INTRODUCTION

Michael Pollan got it right (and, let's be honest, inspired a ton of people) with his very simple, accessible food philosophy: "Eat food. Not too much. Mostly plants." I humbly add one more perspective: Feel good. So often we focus on what we're cutting out or adding in without thinking about the end result: what's good for us isn't solely reflected by a low calorie or carbohydrate count. It's captured in how we feel.

After graduating from college in 2012, I worked a job with long hours (still do) and bought most of my meals instead of making them—from a vending machine, from the drive-through, and from restaurants. It was the most efficient way to get food into my body but I didn't feel good, or good about myself, after eating that way. I'd convinced myself that I didn't have time to cook my own meals or go to the gym. But through the influence of a friend, I changed the foods I ate and my routine.

I started my blog, Cave Girl in the City, to chronicle my culinary adventures following a Paleo diet. Paleo appealed to me because it set a strict guide for what I could and couldn't eat. I cut processed foods out of my diet completely. In time, I learned what did and did not work for my body. I've continued to modify my diet to incorporate the things that make me feel good, and cut out the things that don't.

Confession: I was never particularly skilled in the kitchen. It takes time to cook meals from scratch, which can be a real deterrent. Spiralizers make it ridiculously easy to prepare and eat more vegetables. And even the newest home cook can't help but feel proud when looking down at a colorful, beautiful pile of noodles, produced in seconds. Using a spiralizer helps me enjoy cooking, which allows me continue to eat healthy. Yes, food processors make prep fast and mandolines cut great veggie sticks. But there's something about a tangle of veggie noodles that's not just good for you, it's fun, too.

This is a cookbook for everyone—from those who eat everything to those who can't eat many things. It offers over 100 recipes for the one thing we all need to eat more of: vegetables. Eating healthy does not need to be complicated. Start slow. Eat food. Mostly (spiralized) plants. Feel good.

the tangled table

THERE IS SOMETHING INHERENTLY PLAYFUL about brightly colored, tangled vegetable noodles piled high on your plate. They are beautiful to look at, fun to twirl on your fork, and make a healthy and delicious base for just about any meal you can imagine. Topped with Grandma's tomato sauce, stirred into chicken soup, or even formed into a savory waffle—the options are infinite.

Before we get to the tasty recipes—or what I call "the good stuff"— let's talk about the kitchen tools you need to make vegetable noodles, which vegetables are best for spiralizing, and my tips and tricks for making the most of your tangled table.

The Little Appliance That Could (and Will)

Truth be told, a spiralizer (also known as a spiral slicer) looks a bit like a small torture device. Don't be scared by this; it will transform the way you cook. Once considered a tool merely for creating garnishes, spiralizers have come into the spotlight in recent years for all of the ways they make vegetables more appealing and accessible. From picky kids to raw foodists to the Paleo proud, a spiralizer benefits everyone by expanding—and making more interesting—what you eat.

Still deciding? A spiralizer can also help you:

- **ENJOY YOUR FAVORITE PASTA AND RICE DISHES.** By swapping vegetable noodles for traditional noodles, you can still indulge in your favorite comfort foods like Spaghetti alla Carbonara (page 44), Macaroni & Cheese (page 35), and Spaghetti & Meatballs (page 30) without the guilt (and blood sugar spike) of an intensely carb-heavy meal or the discomfort that gluten wreaks on some bodies. How? Sauces. Have you ever raved about how tasty a macaroni noodle is? Probably not. Macaroni is simply a vehicle for the sauce—and one without taste. You won't miss it.

- **GET THE WHOLE FAMILY INVOLVED.** Spiralizing is not only a great way to get your kids, your other half, or any veggie-reluctant eater you love to give veggies a shot, it's also a great way to engage them in the kitchen. Watching ordinary vegetables magically turn into noodles is fun for everyone—just be careful to supervise children, as those blades are sharp. Very sharp.

- **MAKE MEAL PREP A BREEZE.** Everyone is busy, so why add to the stress of getting a healthy meal on the table? Spiralizing a vegetable generally takes less than 60 seconds and then only a few minutes to cook. You can save even more time by spiralizing your vegetables in advance.

- **TRY NEW THINGS.** While familiar vegetables like carrots, sweet potatoes, and zucchini make flavorful vegetable noodles, you can spiralize a wide variety of other vegetables as well. Spiralizing less common vegetables, like daikon radish, jicama, and kohlrabi, is an easy way to expand your palate and learn about new foods you may not have cooked with before.

- **SIGNIFICANTLY UP YOUR VEGGIE INTAKE.** Spiralizing is an appealing and simple way to meet—and possibly exceed—your recommended daily servings of vegetables. After all, no matter what our dietary restrictions are, we all strive to eat more vegetables. By adding veggie noodles and veggie rice to your meals you will easily satisfy the suggested intake without thinking twice.

Choose Your Noodler

If you're a card-carrying member of the Spiralizer Nation, you may already know a lot about spiralizer options. You might want to jump ahead in the chapter to where I talk about making the most of your spiralizer with a range of produce (see page 18). For beginners and as a refresher for others, reviewing your options never hurts. So, here's what the spiralizer market has to offer.

Though relatively inexpensive compared with some other kitchen tools, spiralizers can range from $10 to $50. When determining which spiralizer is right for you, consider how often you will use it, how much you want to spend, and the variety of noodle shapes you intend to make.

While many brands are available, all spiralizers fall into two main categories: Hand-crank models, or hourglass models. These are not official terms, but once I explain each category, you will understand why I chose these descriptors.

Hand-Crank Model

Hand-crank models are about the size of a toaster and use a crank handle, similar to an old-fashioned apple peeler. They're a cinch to use and, best of all, their multi-blade options give you the widest variety of spiralized noodles.

How It Works

The fruit or vegetable is held in place between small prongs on the handle and on the central coring blade. As you turn the handle, the vegetable is pushed through the blade, creating a pile of extra-long, gently curled ribbons.

The Pros

- **EASY TO CLEAN:** Most hand-crank models are dishwasher safe and also easy to clean with a small hand brush, soap, and water.

- **EASY TO USE:** The hand-crank design quickly churns out vegetable noodles with minimal effort.

- **MORE NOODLE OPTIONS:** Hand-crank models come with three or four interchangeable blade options to create different sizes of noodles, including flat spiral ribbons, thick fettuccine noodles, and thin spaghetti noodles. I find that the hand-crank models not only offer a wider variety of shapes, but also their noodles look better than those produced by hourglass models.

- **PRECISION AND CONTROL:** Suction cups on the base of the spiralizer keep it steady, offering increased leverage and ease of spiralizing.

The Cons

- **LARGE FOOTPRINT:** Much larger than their hourglass counterparts, hand-crank models are about the size of a toaster, taking up considerable cabinet or counter space.

- **COST:** Hand-crank models retail for $30 to $50, a larger investment than the hourglass alternative.

Best Vegetables

- Most hand-crank models can accommodate fruit and vegetables up to 10 inches long and 7 inches thick, meaning it can tackle all spiralizable fruits or veggies. They are ideal for large, tough root vegetables like beets, potatoes, and squash that cannot be spiralized with an hourglass model.

Popular Brands

- The Inspiralizer
- Paderno World Cuisine Tri-Blade Spiral Vegetable Slicer
- Spiralizer Tri-Blade Vegetable Spiral Slicer
- Sur La Table's Vegetable and Fruit Spiral Slicer

Hourglass Model

Hourglass spiralizers are small and extremely lightweight. They take up little space in a kitchen drawer and are entirely portable, making them a great option for anyone on the go. Why not make fresh vegetable noodles at work for a quick and nutritious salad?

How It Works

The hourglass model is the simplest and least expensive spiralizer on the market. It functions like a giant pencil sharpener. Each end of the spiralizer produces a different size noodle. Simply place the vegetable into one end and twist. When the vegetable gets very short, use the cap to twist the remaining vegetable to reduce waste.

The Pros

- **EASY TO CLEAN:** Like its larger counterpart, most hourglass models are dishwasher safe and also easy to clean with soap and water.

- **EASY TO STORE:** Due to their compact size, these spiralizers are small enough to store in a kitchen drawer, making them ideal for those with small kitchens and/or limited storage space.

- **INEXPENSIVE:** Most hourglass models retail for under $20, a smaller investment for first-time users or those who, perhaps, may not spiralize often enough to justify a pricier hand-crank model.

The Cons

- **DIFFICULT TO NOODLE:** Although relatively straightforward in concept, the hourglass model requires a bit of effort to produce long vegetable noodles.

- **SHORTER NOODLES:** Hourglass models offer only two noodle sizes and the noodles produced are often much shorter shreds than those produced by the hand-crank model. You can technically ring out spaghetti-shaped noodles but the noodles won't resemble real spaghetti as much as those that come out of the hand-crank spiralizers.

Best Vegetables

Hourglass-style spiralizers work best with long, thin vegetables, such as carrots, cucumbers, and zucchini. However, you can cut larger vegetables into smaller slices so they fit into the spiralizer.

Popular Brands

- Brieftons Spiral Slicer
- GEFU Spirelli Spiral Slicer
- Kitchen Active Spiralizer Spiral Slicer
- Veggetti

Brieftons NextGen Spiralizer

SAFETY FIRST

It's important to remember that spiral slicers produce beautiful long vegetable noodles thanks to their super-sharp stainless steel blades. As with any sharp object, safety considerations are key when handling these kitchen tools created to slice and dice, and which are just as capable of slicing fingers as carrots. I've suffered my share of nicks and cuts to prove it.

Take special care when handling the hand-crank model blades, especially when placing them into the spiralizer, when removing them, and when cleaning them.

The central coring blade on hand-crank models can also be extremely sharp. When you have finished spiralizing, use either a knife to remove the leftover vegetable from the coring blade or a high-pressure stream of water to wash away excess vegetable slices.

When it comes to handling and cleaning hourglass models, most have finger guards in place but it is still important to pay attention to keep hands safe.

What about Julienne Peelers and Mandolines?

Spiralizers are having their moment, but are they worth the hype? What about other kitchen appliances that can produce vegetable noodles? Here's an overview of what spiralizers, julienne peelers, and mandolines can bring to your tangled table.

SPIRALIZERS: There is no question that spiralizers make the best-looking vegetable noodles and, for many of us, the better our food looks (especially food-for-you food), the more likely we are to devour it. But looks aren't everything. It's important to weigh the cost and storage space required for these kitchen tools against how often you will use them and what types of noodle dishes you want to prepare.

If looking at a beautiful plate of vegetable noodles inspires you to stick to a regular, healthy, and vegetable-full diet, a spiralizer is definitely worth the investment. Motivation is a factor you can't ignore. A hand-crank spiralizer will offer you the most variety in terms of the range of vegetables you can turn into noodles (and, in some cases, rice).

JULIENNE PEELERS: Julienne peelers are a fantastic kitchen tool that can help you create quick and easy vegetable noodles. They look and function much like a vegetable peeler—maybe you even purchased one when you intended to buy a simple peeler. (No? That was just me then!) The easiest way to tell the difference is that a julienne peeler has small micro blades that cut whatever you are peeling into very thin, matchstick-like strips resembling short pieces of spaghetti.

Many recipes in this book call for ribboned noodles, which are impossible to create on a julienne peeler. But just between us, there's no reason you can't use a julienne peeler to make a spaghetti noodle shape instead.

Using a julienne peeler is relatively simple, but it often produces much more waste than a spiralizer. But clean up couldn't be easier. Just rinse the peeler under a stream of water, using soap and a small brush when needed.

Julienne peelers retail from $5 to $15 and can be found at just about any home goods store. While most of the less expensive versions (like the OXO brand) work well, I prefer the all-metal version by Kuhn Rikon.

MANDOLINES: This simple device has long been popular for quickly and effortlessly producing long thin cuts and shavings of your favorite vegetables. Because many recipes in this book call for ribboned noodles, which mandolines can't make, this tool is not the

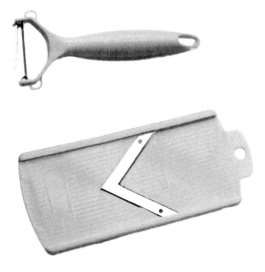

FOR THE LOVE OF BROCCOLI

Broccoli is an unsung vegetable in the world of spiralizing—but we're about to change that.

Most people think the broccoli florets are all that's worth eating of broccoli, and easy-to-buy, easy-to-use pre-packaged bags of broccoli florets don't help change that notion. Of course, you can't spiralize florets. But for those looking to put their spiralizers to the test with as many different vegetables as possible, look no further than the long, thick, and flavorful stem on which those florets grow.

The hitch: you need a broccoli bunch with a wide enough stem. Train your eyes to recognize those that are at least 1½ inches in diameter, and as straight and long as possible. It can be difficult to find these in larger grocery stores, where products (even produce) tend to cater to the masses and mass preferences—such as florets. I have found the best broccoli candidates for spiralizing at farmers' markets and grocery stores with large organic produce sections.

The food for sale there tends to resemble more closely how it looks right off the farm.

To prep the broccoli stem for spiralizing: Remove the florets but preserve as much of the stem as possible. Then, cut off the stem ends so they are flat and align evenly into the spiralizer.

One large broccoli stem yields about one cup of noodles. Don't forget about the florets, though—you can cook these along with the broccoli stem noodles to create a flavorful and filling dish.

best choice for those recipes. However, the mandoline works great for making the very thin noodles called for in vegetable lasagnas or for vegetable chips.

Like the spiralizer, the mandoline creates its thin vegetable slices with super-sharp stainless steel blades, so use caution when handling the blades. Most mandolines are dishwasher safe; however, I find they are also easy to clean with a small hand brush, soap, and water.

When I first began experimenting with vegetable noodles, I purchased a combination countertop julienne peeler/mandoline that had interchangeable blades and easily produced matchstick-size noodles and thin vegetable strips. While I still reach for it from time to time to make zucchini lasagna, my spiralizer has the more prominent location on my countertop, and I use it to produce perfectly rounded vegetable noodle dishes every week!

As I mentioned, the recipes in this cookbook were developed using a spiral slicer and are therefore intended for preparation with this tool. That being said, use your imagination—and available equipment—to adapt these recipes to other vegetable cuts.

All the Produce That's Fit to Noodle

Once you begin brainstorming ways to use the spiralizer in your day-to-day life, you will undoubtedly come to a point where you wonder whether your favorite foods can be spiralized. (Unfortunately, that will not include dark chocolate, raw cheeses, or grilled steaks.) Spiralizers are specifically designed to spiralize *produce* and, despite my best efforts, even some produce is not fit to noodle. In fact, after quite a bit of time in the test kitchen, I can confidently share with you the characteristics that distinguish a fruit or vegetable as a good candidate for spiralizing from those that will fall flat—or produce a big pile of mush.

For best results, the fruit or vegetable should be:

- Firm
- Seedless, and contain no core or pit
- Ripe
- At least 1½ inches wide
- At least 2 inches long

So in the heat of summer, at the height of tomato season, grab your chef's knife, because tomatoes just aren't the spiralizer's thing. Most fruits, sadly, are not great candidates for spiralizing either. Your best bet is to stick with apples and pears.

With every rule come exceptions. Here are two:

EGGPLANT—SKIP IT. You might expect eggplant to be an optimal candidate for the spiralizer. After all, it has a firm flesh, no core, and is a sufficiently large size. However, the reality is that eggplant is very difficult to spiralize—arm-achingly difficult—and, worst of all, does not yield usable noodles.

BELL PEPPER—SPIRALIZE IT. It's completely reasonable to expect that a bell pepper, both hollow and full of seeds, would not noodle. Hand-crank spiralizers, however, produce long, crunchy bell pepper noodles that are perfect for frittatas and stir-fries. Bell pepper lovers need only chop off the stem and affix the top of the pepper to the spiralizer combs (bottom goes on the corer). Just be prepared to clean up the mess produced by the mass of seeds within the pepper's hollow center.

Getting Started

Most fruits and vegetables require minimal prep before spiralizing. Most important to do is remove stems and cut the ends off fruits and vegetables, creating a flat end that fits securely in the spiralizer. Some vegetables will need to be peeled to produce vegetable noodles but, when possible, leave the skin on to retain the maximum nutritional value.

Every recipe in this book provides prep for specific ingredients, but the table on page 20 offers a handy guide to prepping commonly used produce.

From Noodles to Rice or Sandwiches

Like traditional noodles, vegetable noodles are versatile. They can quickly transition from pasta to "rice," and even buns and bagels.

RICE: With a mini food processor, spiralized rice is a cinch to prepare and can replace white and brown rice, or other grains, in your favorite dishes. You can eat it raw, sautéed, or even baked in a casserole or frittata. By ricing vegetable noodles, you can make many of the grain-free recipes in this book, including Pork Fried Rice (page 39), Broccoli & Egg Hash Brown Cups (page 50), Potato & Turnip Gratin (page 71), Squash & Asparagus Risotto (page 103), and Roasted Lamb with Jicama Rice (page 145).

To make vegetable rice, first spiralize the vegetable into noodles. Then add the noodles to a food processor and gently pulse for about 5 seconds, or until a rice-like consistency forms. Almost any ingredient that can be spiralized, can also be turned into spiralized rice.

The *exceptions* include apples, cucumbers, and pears, due to their high water content.

SANDWICHES: Bagels and buns become possible when you spiralize some of the starchier vegetables, such as potatoes and sweet potatoes. Compared with other vegetables, potatoes and sweet potatoes have higher carbohydrate counts, but their carb content is much lower than the traditional bread bun alternative. For clean eaters who enjoy a break every now and again from whole-wheat bread products, vegetable-based buns are a flavorful, filling, and perfectly unprocessed option.

YOUR PRODUCE PREP GUIDE

FRUITS & VEGGIES	PREPARATION	THE GOOD STUFF
Apple	Remove the stem	Fiber and vitamin C
Beet	Remove the ends and peel	Foliate and magnesium
Bell pepper	Remove the stem	Antioxidants and vitamin C
Broccoli stem	Remove the florets and peel	Calcium, fiber, potassium, vitamin C
Butternut squash	Remove the bottom, peel, and halve	Fiber and vitamin A
Cabbage	Remove the outer layers	Vitamins C and K
Carrot	Remove the ends, peel, and halve	Beta-carotene, vitamins A, K, and B_6
Cassava root	Remove the ends and peel	Calcium, vitamin C
Celeriac (celery root)	Remove the ends and peel	Phosphorus, vitamins C and K
Chayote	Remove the ends and halve	Foliate, potassium, vitamin C
Cucumber	Remove the ends, halve, and remove excess moisture with a kitchen towel	Fiber and vitamin K
Daikon radish	Remove the ends, peel, and halve	Fiber and vitamin C
Jicama	Remove the ends, peel, and halve	Fiber and vitamin C
Kohlrabi	Remove the ends, peel, and halve	Fiber and vitamin C
Onion	Remove the outer layers and ends	Manganese and vitamin C
Parsnip	Remove the ends, peel, and halve	Fiber, folic acid, and vitamin C
Pear	Remove the ends	Fiber and vitamin C
Plantain	Remove the ends, peel, and halve	Potassium, vitamins A, B_6, and C
Potato	Remove the ends and peel	Fiber, vitamins B_6 and C
Radicchio	Remove the outer layers	Folic acid, vitamins B_6 and K
Radish	Remove the ends	Vitamin C
Rutabaga	Remove the ends, peel, and halve	Vitamin C
Summer squash	Remove the ends	Fiber, foliate, potassium, vitamins A, C
Sweet potato	Remove the ends and peel	Beta-carotene, fiber, vitamins A and C
Taro root	Remove the ends and peel	Fiber
Turnip	Remove the ends and peel	Vitamin C
Zucchini	Remove the ends	Fiber, foliate, potassium, vitamins A, C

THERE'S A SAUCE FOR THAT

Just as dressings are what make salads sing, sauces are what give pastas and rice dishes the flavors that make them memorable.

If you're unsure how to pair vegetables with sauces and herbs, don't worry—there is no set formula. Let the taste, texture, and heartiness of the vegetables, and your palate, be your guide. Use the suggestions here to inspire your vegetable noodle creations.

Beets have a strong earthy flavor that is not overwhelmed by flavorful sauces such as creamy nut-based sauces and caramelized syrups and glazes.

Broccoli stems have a mild character that will not compete with a variety of flavorful sauces, such as marinara or stir-fry sauces, as well as with olive oil–based or creamy dressings.

Carrots are naturally sweet, so they work well with simple, light sauces and glazes—from peanut sauces to teriyaki sauces that complement but don't overwhelm their taste.

Celeriac has a tart, herbal flavor reminiscent of celery stalks. Spiralized into sturdy noodles, celeriac provides a good match to hold thick Italian sauces such as carbonara and Bolognese.

Jicama's lightly sweet, nutty flavor and crisp texture pair successfully with oil-based dressings and vinaigrettes. Jicama noodles are also tasty when eaten raw.

Sweet potatoes, naturally sweet like carrots, also absorb liquids so they stand up to heavier, creamy and nut-based sauces.

Turnips have a bitter taste that is easily masked by bold, flavorful sauces and dressings such as pesto.

Zucchini and summer squash are mild in flavor and can be used in a variety of ways. As vegetable noodles, they pair with both light and heavy sauces. They're also delicious enjoyed on their own.

Pass on Pesticides

Don't compromise the effort you're making to eat fruit- and vegetable-based meals. Make the most of their nutritious benefits by buying the healthiest produce available—sometimes this means buying only organic, and in some cases conventionally-farmed produce is fine.

Each year the Environmental Working Group (EWG) analyzes the pesticide residue in fruits and vegetables, testing data from the US Food and Drug Administration. For years, the EWG has published the "Dirty Dozen," which identifies the 12 fruits and vegetables with the highest pesticide residue; these days, it is known as the "Dirty Dozen Plus" because the count now totals 14. Because these foods, when farmed conventionally, contain undesirably high levels of pesticides, it's best to only purchase them if you can find them organic.

Alternately, the "Clean 15" list identifies conventionally-farmed produce that contains the *least* amount of pesticide residue, so it's not as necessary to buy these items organic every time.

From the list of fruits and vegetables that can be spiralized (see page 20), there are only a few items on the "Dirty Dozen" list: apples, cucumbers, and potatoes. For more information about the "Dirty Dozen" and "Clean 15," see the full list on page 181.

Supporting Kitchen Equipment

Learning to cook a balanced, healthy meal was one of the most daunting, yet rewarding, experiences of my clean-eating journey. But here's a secret: you don't need a kitchen full of fancy tools to be a good cook. In fact, I bet you already have several of the eight items I consider essential for cooking, in general, and complementing the work of your spiralizer.

CAST IRON SKILLET: A cast iron skillet has a natural nonstick bottom, heats evenly, can be transferred to the oven, and will last forever if you care for it properly. Equally adept at sautéing vegetable noodles, searing meat, and cooking eggs, this tool is a must-have for every kitchen. A few tips for keeping your cast iron skillet in tip-top shape: season with oil before use; always wash it without using soap; and keep it dry so it doesn't rust. Unfortunately, it's easy to ruin cast iron so, at the very least, we can be grateful it's afford-able to replace. You can purchase an 8-inch cast iron skillet online for just under $11.

CHEF'S KNIFE. A dull knife is not only difficult to use but a hazard in the kitchen. Invest in a quality chef's knife that will chop the ends off tough root vegetables with ease.

CUTTING BOARD: When prepping vegetables for the spiralizer, a cutting board will be your best friend. Stick with a plastic or wooden board, as these will be easiest on your new chef's knife.

FOOD PROCESSOR: If you want to make spiralized rice recipes, you'll need a food processor, but nothing elaborate. An inexpensive mini food processor is sufficient to get the job done.

GLASS BAKING DISHES: These dishes are perfect for roasting root vegetables and can also double as food storage containers. They're great for storing and reheating spiralized dishes when heading to a family party or bringing leftovers to work.

KITCHEN SCISSORS: Once you get the hang of spiralizing, you'll be creating exquisitely long vegetable noodles in no time. While they are impressive to look at, they can be difficult to eat (remember *Lady and the Tramp*?). So, run a pair of kitchen scissors through your freshly spiralized noodles to make them a bit more manageable in size before cooking.

KITCHEN TONGS: Tongs are essential when cooking spiralized foods, tossing them with sauce, and moving them from skillet to plate. Stick with a simple, inexpensive pair—as long as you are gentle, both metal and rubber versions work fine.

VEGETABLE PEELER: Although the skin should be left intact on fruits, many vegetables need to be peeled before being spiralized. Rather than risk injury with your sharp new chef's knife, a good-quality vegetable peeler will help you battle those tough vegetable exteriors.

Five Tips for Budding Spiralistas

Raring to get started? Maybe you've already purchased a brand new spiralizer. Perhaps you've even jumped ahead and already spiralized your first zucchini. If so, that's great. But before you jump into the recipes and never look back, I want to share my top tips for making the most of your vegetable noodles.

1. **PICK THE LARGEST VEGETABLES.** Spiralizing fruits and veggies that are short and barely meet the minimum diameter requirement not only yields fewer noodles but also half-moon scraps instead of long noodle ribbons. For best results select the largest, thickest vegetables you can find and center them on the spiralizer. Shopping seasonally is the best way to find extra-large veggies that will spiralize with ease.

2. **PREP YOUR VEGGIE NOODLES IN ADVANCE.** Planning and prepping meals over the weekend can vastly cut your time making food throughout the week. Do one big prep, spiralizing butternut squash, cucumber, sweet potato, and zucchini noodles in advance, and store the vegetables in airtight containers. Not only will this save you time but also cut down the number of dishes used and overall clean-up time.

THE ZUCCHINI IN THE ROOM

Zucchini are without a doubt the front-runner of "spiralizable" vegetables. I had seen *zoodles* gracing the blogosphere long before I purchased my first spiralizer, and for good reason: zucchini are chock-full of potassium, foliate, and vitamin A, all vital nutrients for overall good health, as well as being extremely versatile when it comes to preparation.

Zoodles have long been touted as an excellent replacement for traditional noodles in pasta recipes, but they can also be turned into a number of other tasty dishes. So, how can you make the most of your spiralized zucchini? Let's talk about how to prep, store, and cook zucchini noodles for optimum results.

Preparation: Peeling zucchini prior to spiralizing is optional based on preference; however, it is important to note that due to zucchini's high water content, the vast majority of nutrients are stored in its skin. Therefore, I leave the skin on in many zucchini dishes, making prep a breeze. After you rinse the zucchini, simply slice off each end so both sides are flat and even.

Storage: Zucchini noodles can be prepared in advance and refrigerated in an airtight container for up to 5 days, but they should not be frozen.

Cooking: Serve zucchini noodles raw, boiled (2 to 3 minutes), or sautéed (2 to 3 minutes). They can also be roasted in a frittata or casserole along with other vegetable noodles. Zucchini noodles make an appearance in a number of recipes throughout this cookbook, including soups, salads, and even dessert. Some of my favorites are Chicken Zoodle Soup (page 34), Chocolate-Zucchini Muffins (page 52), and Zucchini Ribbon Crisp (page 169). With such an abundance of zucchini-inspired flavor to choose from, which recipe will you try first?

3. **AVOID WATERY NOODLES.** Given that most vegetables contain a fair amount of water, it is inevitable that your vegetable noodles will release water when cooked (some more than others). Avoid letting the noodles sit in sauce for long periods of time. Cook the noodles in a separate skillet from the sauce, and join them right before serving. If you spiralize more noodles than you plan to use, reserve the noodles and store separately from the sauce.

4. **SAVE THE SCRAPS.** The one downside of spiralizing some vegetables is that they leave behind perfectly usable vegetable scraps, which is often the case, for example, with broccoli florets and butternut squash bottoms. Instead of wasting these perfectly good vegetables, save scraps for homemade broth, or simply dice them and incorporate them into your dish.

5. **CLEAN YOUR SPIRALIZER RIGHT AFTER USE.** Spiralizers are easy to clean if done soon after you've finished spiralizing. A small hand brush is essential and makes the clean-up task simple and safe. Use the brush with soap and water to clean the spiralizer after each use. The natural coloring in some vegetables, like beets, carrots, and sweet potatoes, may discolor your spiralizer, but you can combat this with soap and water, as well. Most spiralizers are also dishwasher safe, but your blades will last longest if you hand wash them.

This Book's Recipes

Now let's get to the good stuff: 96 tasty, tangled noodle recipes designed to kick-start your spiralizing journey, plus 12 sauces and condiments to flavor your noodles and any other type of meal you choose.

Dietary Requirements

As I mentioned earlier, one of the best things about a spiralizer is that it works for each and every one of us, regardless of dietary restrictions, which is great because these days it feels like everyone is trying to eat less processed food and add more real, whole food to their diet. That said, many people do follow specific guidelines and approaches to clean eating (whether it's all of the time or most of the time). I include recipe labels throughout the book to indicate whether a recipe is **DAIRY FREE, GLUTEN FREE, PALEO, VEGAN,** or **VEGETARIAN.**

Because we all don't follow the same diet, some recipes include two options for an ingredient—for example, whole milk or almond milk. You choose the ingredient that works for you. In a case like the one noted, the recipe will be labeled *dairy free* because it gives a dairy-free option, even though the other option contains dairy. Here are some other options you'll see throughout:

- soy sauce or coconut aminos (soy sauce is not gluten-free, coconut aminos is)

- all-purpose flour or coconut flour (all-purpose flour is not gluten-free, coconut flour is)

- butter or grass-fed butter (those who follow the Paleo diet can eat butter from grass-fed cows)

As my diet is primarily free of dairy and 100 percent free of gluten, I prepared and tested the recipes with the ingredients that fit the way that I eat, but I've gone ahead and included more common ingredient options for those whose diets aren't as restrictive.

Making the Cut

When I first started using my spiralizer, I occasionally looked online for recipes and got frustrated when they would simply say to spiralize an ingredient, but not indicate what the spiralized noodle should look like. Recipes in this book always note which noodle shape you should shoot for:

RIBBONED NOODLES (see opposite page, top): these are the flat noodle shapes, and they can only be made with a hand-crank spiralizer. Use the blade that has no triangles on it. If you only have an hourglass spiralizer, the recipe will still work, unless it's a lasagna recipe.

FETTUCCINE-SHAPED NOODLES (see opposite page, middle): these are the thicker, round noodle shapes, and can be made with a hand-crank spiralizer or an hourglass spiralizer. With the hand-crank, use the blade with larger, fewer triangles. With the hourglass, add the vegetable to the side labeled "thick," or with the blade combs farther apart.

SPAGHETTI-SHAPED NOODLES (see opposite page, bottom): these are the thinner, round noodle shapes, and can be made with a hand-crank spiralizer or an hourglass spiralizer. With the hand-crank, use the blade with the smaller, more numerous triangles. With the hourglass, add the vegetable to the side labeled "thin," or with the combs closer together to produce the thinner noodle.

As you begin, remember to read the recipes through in their entirety, and gather all the ingredients and kitchen tools you will need in advance. Like everything else, a little prep work before you begin cooking will save you time in the long run.

Now that you understand spiralizing basics, it's time to put everything you've been reading into practice. I hope you have as much fun preparing these recipes as I did developing them!

Spaghetti & Meatballs **30**

Chicken Pad Thai **32**

Chicken Zoodle Soup **34**

Macaroni & Cheese **35**

Meat & Veggie Pizza **37**

classic cravings

Pork Fried Rice **39**

Loaded Plantain Nachos **40**

Chicken & Broccoli Fettuccine Alfredo **42**

Spaghetti alla Carbonara **44**

Vegetable Lo Mein **45**

DAIRY FREE, GLUTEN FREE, PALEO

SPAGHETTI
& MEATBALLS

When my boyfriend and I first moved in together, I was nothing short of a disaster in the kitchen, but, yes, I could at least boil a pot of water. Despite my ignorance as a chef, I insisted on Sunday dinners. I cooked the spaghetti, and he took charge of the meatballs and sauce. Although our kitchen skills (and mine in particular) have evolved over the years, our Sunday night dinners endure—only these days we swap the spaghetti for zucchini noodles.

SERVES 4

1 pound ground beef

4 eggs

1 cup finely chopped fresh spinach

½ cup almond meal

4 garlic cloves, minced

1 tablespoon dried oregano

1 tablespoon dried basil

1 tablespoon dried parsley

1 teaspoon onion powder

Sea salt

Freshly ground black pepper

1½ cups Classic Tomato Marinara (page 172)

1½ teaspoons extra-virgin olive oil

2 zucchini, spiralized into spaghetti noodles

VEGETABLE SUBSTITUTION: BEET, CARROT, KOHLRABI, SUMMER SQUASH, SWEET POTATO, TURNIPS

1. Preheat the oven to 350°F and line a baking sheet with parchment paper.

2. In a large bowl, use your hands to mix the ground beef, eggs, spinach, almond meal, garlic, oregano, basil, parsley, and onion powder. Season with sea salt and pepper.

3. Form the meat mixture in 12 meatballs, about golf-ball size, and place them on the prepared sheet. Bake for 25 minutes.

4. When the meatballs are cooked about halfway through, add the Marinara to a small saucepan set over low heat. Cook for about 10 minutes, or until warmed through.

5. Just before the meatballs finish cooking, heat a large skillet over medium-high heat. Add the olive oil and zucchini noodles. Cook for 2 to 3 minutes, tossing, until al dente.

6. Serve the zucchini noodles topped with the Marinara and meatballs.

PREP TIP: *I like to peel the zucchini for this dish so the noodles resemble a traditional bowl of pasta.*

PER SERVING: CALORIES: 433; FAT: 23G; TOTAL CARBOHYDRATES: 13G; FIBER: 4G; PROTEIN: 45G

CHICKEN
PAD THAI

Every now and again I get an overwhelming craving for pad thai. There is just something irresistible about that perfect balance of sweet, salty, and tart. So, I decided to turn my uncontrollable need for my favorite Thai takeout dish into something positive by making a much healthier, veggie-packed version. Add a little fun to the table by serving this dish in takeout boxes with chopsticks.

SERVES 4

FOR THE SAUCE

4 tablespoons freshly squeezed lime juice

4 tablespoons soy sauce or coconut aminos

3 tablespoons chili sauce

2 tablespoons fish sauce

2 tablespoons raw honey

2 teaspoons red pepper flakes

1 tablespoon sesame oil

FOR THE PAD THAI

2 eggs

1 tablespoon sesame oil

1 pound boneless skinless chicken breast, cut into thin strips

4 large carrots, spiralized into spaghetti noodles

1 red bell pepper, spiralized into spaghetti noodles

3 scallions, sliced thin

1 garlic clove, minced

1 tablespoon all-purpose flour or coconut flour

½ red cabbage, spiralized into spaghetti-like strands

1 teaspoon sesame seeds

VEGETABLE SUBSTITUTION: BROCCOLI STEM, DAIKON RADISH, SUMMER SQUASH, SWEET POTATO

1. In a small bowl, stir together the lime juice, soy sauce, chili sauce, fish sauce, honey, red pepper flakes, and sesame oil. Set aside.

2. In a large skillet set over medium heat, scramble the eggs. Remove them from the skillet and set aside.

3. Return the skillet to medium heat. Add the sesame oil. Once the oil is heated, add the chicken. Cook for 5 minutes, or until cooked through. Remove the chicken from the skillet and set aside with the eggs.

4. Reduce the heat under the skillet to low. Add the carrot and red bell pepper noodles. Cook for 3 to 5 minutes. Remove the noodles from the skillet and set aside.

5. Add the scallions and garlic to the skillet. Cook for 2 to 3 minutes, stirring constantly. Once the scallions begin to soften, add the sauce to the skillet. Add the flour slowly, whisking until the sauce begins to thicken. Add the carrot and bell pepper noodles back to the skillet and toss to coat. Finally, add the chicken, scrambled eggs, and cabbage noodles.

6. Garnish with sesame seeds and serve.

PER SERVING: CALORIES: 420; FAT: 18G; TOTAL CARBOHYDRATES: 25G; FIBER: 4G; PROTEIN: 39G

CHICKEN
ZOODLE SOUP

SPIRALIZE IT!

From the time I was a little girl I've been convinced of the healing powers of chicken soup. After all, when I had my wisdom teeth out and couldn't eat solid foods, it was chicken soup that came to the rescue. Even now, when I'm just having a bad day, sitting down to a steamy bowl can definitely turn things around.

SERVES 4

- 1 white onion, diced
- 2 celery stalks, diced
- 2 carrots, diced
- **2 zucchini**, spiralized into spaghetti noodles
- 1 teaspoon apple cider vinegar
- 1 tablespoon Herbes de Provence
- 1 pound boneless skinless chicken breast
- 1 teaspoon sea salt
- ½ teaspoon freshly ground black pepper
- 2 cups chicken broth
- 2 cups water

VEGETABLE SUBSTITUTION: BROCCOLI STEM, CELERIAC, DAIKON RADISH, JICAMA, SUMMER SQUASH, TURNIP

1. In a slow cooker, layer the onion, celery, and carrots, followed by the zucchini noodles.

2. Add the apple cider vinegar and Herbes de Provence.

3. Place the chicken in a single layer on top of the vegetables, and season it with the sea salt and the pepper.

4. Slowly pour the chicken broth and water into the cooker. Cook on low for 7 hours.

5. After cooking, remove the chicken and shred it with two forks. Return the chicken to the soup, stir to combine, and serve.

PER SERVING: CALORIES: 275; FAT: 3G; TOTAL CARBOHYDRATES: 10G; FIBER: 3G; PROTEIN: 37G

MACARONI &
CHEESE

Macaroni and cheese has long been touted as the ultimate kid food—it was my top pick. Whether homemade with fresh cheese and crunchy panko bread crumbs or straight from the box, I didn't care as long as the noodles were covered in cheese sauce. When I gave up grains and dairy I missed this childhood favorite. I began reintroducing high-quality dairy back into my diet about a year ago, and found I can tolerate raw cheese from cows, in moderation. This recipe is definitely a treat in my house and provides a great way to satisfy a carb-heavy craving with healthy vegetables.

SERVES 4

- 1½ teaspoons extra-virgin olive oil or coconut oil
- 1 cup full-fat coconut milk
- ¼ teaspoon sea salt
- ¼ teaspoon freshly ground black pepper
- ½ cup vegetable broth
- 2 tablespoons all-purpose flour or coconut flour
- 1 egg
- 1 jicama, spiralized into spaghetti noodles
- 2 cups shredded Cheddar cheese

VEGETABLE SUBSTITUTION: BUTTERNUT SQUASH, CARROT, SUMMER SQUASH, SWEET POTATO, TURNIP

1. Preheat the oven to 350°F, and then grease an 8-inch-by-8-inch oven-safe baking dish with the olive oil.

2. Place a skillet over medium heat. Add the coconut milk, sea salt, and pepper. Cook for 2 to 3 minutes, or until heated through. Stir in the vegetable broth. While continuing to stir, add the flour and mix well to combine.

3. Bring the sauce to a boil and then remove the skillet from the heat. Add the egg to the skillet and whisk until thickened.

4. At the bottom of the baking dish, layer the jicama noodles. Pour the sauce over the jicama, and then cover with the cheese.

5. Place the dish in the oven and bake for about 45 minutes.

6. Turn the oven to broil. Broil for 3 to 5 minutes, or until the cheese begins to turn golden brown.

PER SERVING: CALORIES: 460; FAT: 34G; TOTAL CARBOHYDRATES: 21G; FIBER: 8G; PROTEIN: 19G

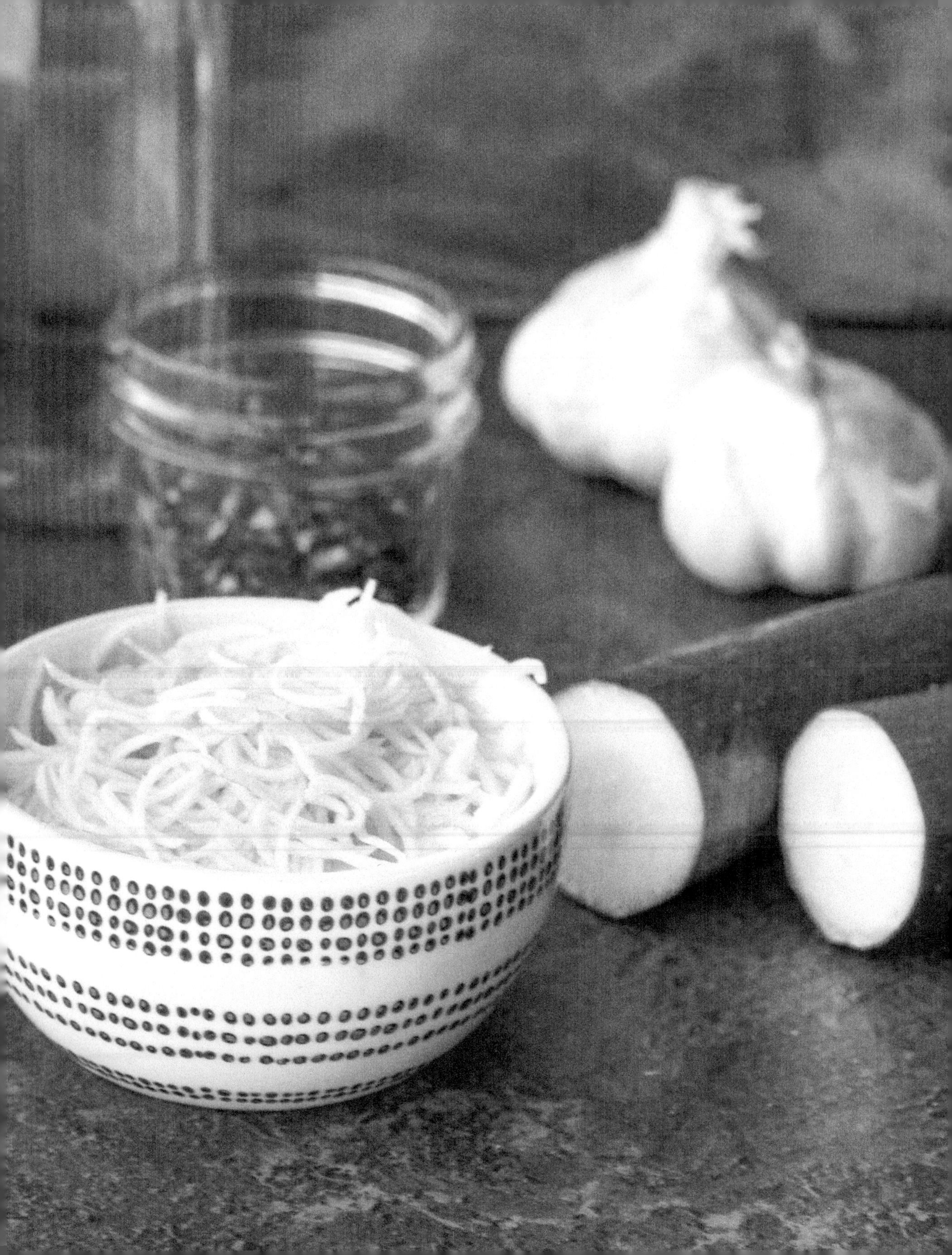

HONEY-SESAME BROCCOLI
SALAD

DAIRY FREE, GLUTEN FREE, PALEO, VEGETARIAN

A variation of traditional coleslaw, broccoli slaw substitutes shredded raw broccoli for cabbage, and this honey-sesame seasoning takes first prize. The hearty spiralized broccoli stems are far easier to achieve than shredded broccoli, and its flavorful crunch is sure to be a hit with your family.

SERVES 4

2 broccoli stems, spiralized into spaghetti noodles

2 carrots, spiralized into spaghetti noodles

½ cup extra-virgin olive oil

2 tablespoons soy sauce or coconut aminos

2 tablespoons rice wine vinegar

1 tablespoon raw honey

½ teaspoon garlic powder

½ teaspoon ground ginger

¼ teaspoon sea salt

½ cup dried cranberries

2 tablespoons sesame seeds

VEGETABLE SUBSTITUTION: CUCUMBER

1. In a large bowl, toss together the broccoli noodles, carrot noodles, olive oil, soy sauce, rice wine vinegar, honey, garlic powder, ground ginger, and sea salt.

2. Let the salad sit for 30 minutes so the flavors develop.

3. Top with the cranberries and sesame seeds before serving.

PER SERVING: CALORIES: 304; FAT: 28G; TOTAL CARBOHYDRATES: 14G; FIBER: 3G; PROTEIN: 3G

KALE
HARVEST VEGETABLE SALAD

DAIRY FREE, GLUTEN FREE, PALEO, VEGAN

A lot of people shrug off salads as either boring or not enough substance, but this salad has all that and more. A healthy and delicious meal on its own, this salad is sure to satisfy—and is chock-full of nutrients, too.

SERVES 4

- 4 cups chopped kale leaves, thoroughly washed and stemmed
- 4 tablespoons extra-virgin olive oil, divided
- Sea salt
- Freshly ground black pepper
- **1 sweet potato**, spiralized into spaghetti noodles
- 1 teaspoon ground cinnamon
- **1 apple**, spiralized into spaghetti noodles
- ½ cup chopped walnuts
- 2 tablespoons Simple Apple Vinaigrette (page 177)

VEGETABLE SUBSTITUTION: BUTTERNUT SQUASH, CARROT

FRUIT SUBSTITUTION: CHAYOTE, PEAR

1. Preheat the oven to 400°F, and then line 2 baking sheets with parchment paper.

2. In a large bowl, combine the kale and 2 tablespoons of olive oil. Season with sea salt and pepper. Toss well and massage the oil into the kale for 2 minutes.

3. Spread the kale on one of the prepared sheets. Bake for 15 minutes, tossing halfway through. Remove from the oven and set aside.

4. In a small bowl, combine the sweet potato noodles, the remaining 2 tablespoons of olive oil, and the cinnamon. Mix well.

5. Spread the sweet potato mixture on the second prepared sheet. Bake for 8 to 10 minutes.

6. Remove the sheet from the oven and add the apple noodles and walnuts to the sweet potato noodles. Toss and bake for 5 to 8 minutes more, or until lightly browned.

7. In another large bowl, toss together the cooked kale and cooked sweet potato noodle mixture. Drizzle with the Vinaigrette and serve.

PER SERVING: CALORIES: 336; FAT: 27G; TOTAL CARBOHYDRATES: 21G; FIBER: 4G; PROTEIN: 7G

RAW
RAINBOW
NOODLE
SALAD

All spiralized noodles have a striking appearance, but multicolored spiralized noodles together are gorgeous on the plate, tempting your taste buds, and delivering great taste, too. Attractive, delicious, and nutritious—that's what we call a trifecta, my friends.

SERVES 4

- **2 broccoli stems**, spiralized into spaghetti noodles
- **2 carrots**, spiralized into spaghetti noodles
- **1 red beet**, spiralized into spaghetti noodles
- **1 golden beet**, spiralized into spaghetti noodles
- **1 jicama**, spiralized into spaghetti noodles
- ¼ cup chopped almonds
- 2 tablespoons Orange-Basil Vinaigrette (page 176)

VEGETABLE SUBSTITUTION: BELL PEPPER, CELERIAC, CUCUMBER, DAIKON RADISH, ZUCCHINI

1. On a large serving platter, arrange the broccoli noodles, carrot noodles, red beet noodles, golden beet noodles, and jicama noodles into straight lines, grouped by color like a rainbow.

2. Top with the chopped almonds and drizzle with the Vinaigrette before serving.

PER SERVING: CALORIES: 172; FAT: 8G;
TOTAL CARBOHYDRATES: 25G; FIBER: 12G; PROTEIN: 5G

ROASTED CAULIFLOWER
& BEET
SALAD

It never ceases to amaze me how preparation can affect the taste of vegetables—or any food, really. For example, roasting vegetables amplifies their natural sweetness and leaves you wanting more. This recipe pairs earthy beets and cauliflower with peppery arugula for a big bowl of yummy. Turn this salad into a protein-rich meal by adding rotisserie chicken and roasted chickpeas.

SERVES 4

1 **red beet**, spiralized into spaghetti noodles

1 **golden beet**, spiralized into
    spaghetti noodles

1 cauliflower head, trimmed and broken
    into florets

3 cups baby arugula

½ cup halved cherry tomatoes

¼ cup chopped walnuts

2 tablespoons Jalapeño-Lime Vinaigrette
    (page 174)

VEGETABLE SUBSTITUTION: BUTTERNUT
SQUASH, CARROT, DAIKON RADISH, RADISH,
SWEET POTATO

1. Preheat the oven to 400°F, and then line a baking sheet with parchment paper.

2. Arrange the red beet noodles, golden beet noodles, and cauliflower in a single layer on the prepared sheet. Place the sheet in the preheated oven and roast for 20 minutes, tossing halfway through.

3. Turn the oven to broil. Broil for 3 to 5 minutes, or until the beets and cauliflower turn golden brown.

4. In a large bowl, combine the arugula, beets and cauliflower, cherry tomatoes, and walnuts.

5. Drizzle with the Vinaigrette and serve.

PER SERVING: CALORIES: 131; FAT: 9G;
TOTAL CARBOHYDRATES: 11G; FIBER: 4G; PROTEIN: 5G

PEAR,
STRAWBERRY
& GOAT CHEESE
SALAD

Crunchy pears, bright strawberries, and creamy goat cheese put a colorful, fruity spin on this spinach salad. If pears aren't in season, replace them with apples or another seasonal fruit. If you're vegan, Paleo, or dairy-free, leave out the goat cheese.

SERVES 4

- 4 cups baby spinach
- **2 pears**, spiralized into spaghetti noodles
- 8 strawberries, sliced
- ¼ cup crumbled goat cheese
- ¼ cup crushed pecans
- 2 tablespoons Simple Apple Vinaigrette (page 177)

FRUIT SUBSTITUTION: APPLE, CHAYOTE

1. In a large bowl, toss together the spinach, pear noodles, strawberries, goat cheese, and pecans.

2. Drizzle with the Vinaigrette and serve.

MAKE-AHEAD TIP: *Prepare the salad in advance without the pears and salad dressing, and chill. Add the pears and dress the salad just before serving.*

PER SERVING: CALORIES: 236; FAT: 16G; TOTAL CARBOHYDRATES: 21G; FIBER: 5G; PROTEIN: 5G

TOMATO,
CUCUMBER &
AVOCADO
SALAD

This salad screams "summer" and is perfect for when high temperatures call for light, refreshing meals with minimal prep. I tend to use cherry tomatoes in salads because I always seem to have them on hand. When tomatoes are in season, though, I like to use locally grown heirloom tomatoes. Nothing beats a fresh tomato right off the vine. If you can tolerate dairy, or your diet allows it, try this salad topped with crumbled feta cheese.

SERVES 4

1 **cucumber**, spiralized into spaghetti noodles
1 **red onion**, spiralized into spaghetti noodles
½ cup halved cherry tomatoes
1 avocado, diced
2 tablespoons extra-virgin olive oil
1 tablespoon red wine vinegar
¼ cup chopped fresh parsley

VEGETABLE SUBSTITUTION: ZUCCHINI

1. In a large bowl, toss together the cucumber noodles, red onion noodles, cherry tomatoes, and avocado.

2. Drizzle with the olive oil and red wine vinegar. Garnish with parsley before serving.

PER SERVING: CALORIES: 191; FAT: 17G; TOTAL CARBOHYDRATES: 11G; FIBER: 5G; PROTEIN: 2G

VEGGIE & CHICKPEA
SALAD

My favorite days start at the gym. There is something about exercising first thing in the morning that sets me up for a great day both mentally and nutritionally. I keep the momentum going with a healthy, energizing salad at lunch. This is an example of one that makes you feel fantastic inside and out. Filled to the brim with veggies and packed with protein, this salad will power you through the rest of a productive afternoon.

SERVES 2

½ cup chickpeas

1 tablespoon extra-virgin olive oil

1 teaspoon chili powder

½ teaspoon ground cumin

2 carrots, spiralized into spaghetti noodles

1 beet, spiralized into spaghetti noodles

1 broccoli stem, spiralized into spaghetti noodles

¼ cup chopped fresh basil

2 tablespoons Orange-Basil Vinaigrette (page 176)

VEGETABLE SUBSTITUTION: CUCUMBER, DAIKON RADISH, JICAMA, ZUCCHINI

1. Preheat the oven to 400°F, and then line a baking sheet with parchment paper.

2. In a small bowl, toss together the chickpeas, olive oil, chili powder, and cumin. Transfer the mixture to the baking sheet, arranged in a single layer.

3. Place the sheet in the preheated oven and bake for 30 minutes, or until golden brown, tossing occasionally to ensure even roasting.

4. In a large serving bowl, toss together the carrot noodles, beet noodles, broccoli noodles, basil, and chickpeas.

5. Drizzle with the Vinaigrette and serve.

SUBSTITUTION TIP: *Make this salad your own by swapping out the roasted chickpeas for another protein of choice. I like using rotisserie chicken because it requires no prep at all.*

PER SERVING: CALORIES: 399; FAT: 19G; TOTAL CARBOHYDRATES: 49G; FIBER: 14G; PROTEIN: 14G

vegetarian & vegan

COCONUT CURRY
NOODLES

There's something special about curry's welcoming warmth and goodness. This version is chock-full of gorgeous vegetable noodles and spices that are sure to banish the chill of that wintry night or rainy afternoon.

SERVES 4

1 tablespoon coconut oil

1 small white onion, diced

4 garlic cloves, minced

1 teaspoon ground ginger

1 broccoli stem, spiralized into spaghetti noodles

1 large carrot, spiralized into spaghetti noodles

1 daikon radish, spiralized into spaghetti noodles

1 tablespoon curry powder

⅛ teaspoon cayenne pepper, or additional as desired (optional)

2 (13.5-ounce) cans full-fat coconut milk

1¼ cups vegetable broth

Sea salt

Freshly ground black pepper

VEGETABLE SUBSTITUTION: KOHLRABI, PEPPER, ZUCCHINI

1. In a large pot set over medium heat, heat the coconut oil. Add the onion, garlic, ginger, broccoli noodles, carrot noodles, and daikon radish noodles. Stir to combine. Cook for 3 minutes, or until the noodles are tender.

2. Add the curry powder, cayenne pepper (if using), coconut milk, and vegetable broth. Season with sea salt and pepper. Stir to combine.

3. Bring the mixture to a simmer. Reduce the heat to medium-low. Cook for 10 minutes.

4. Serve immediately.

PER SERVING: CALORIES: 525; FAT: 50G; TOTAL CARBOHYDRATES: 20G; FIBER: 7G; PROTEIN: 8G

BUTTERNUT **SQUASH** ENCHILADAS

There's a fantastic Mexican restaurant two blocks from my apartment that satisfies all my Mexican food cravings. But there are times I feel like making enchiladas or other traditional dishes at home. These enchiladas fulfill a dietary triplet of requirements—dairy-free, gluten-free, and vegan—but still serve up irresistible Mexican flavor that is sure to please.

SERVES 4

4 garlic cloves, minced, divided

1 tablespoon extra-virgin olive oil, divided

½ cup tomato sauce

¼ cup vegetable broth

1 tablespoon chipotle chile peppers in adobo sauce

1 teaspoon chili powder, divided

½ teaspoon ground cumin, divided

1 jalapeño pepper, seeded and chopped

1 teaspoon onion powder

1 small butternut squash, spiralized into spaghetti noodles

1 (10-ounce) can diced tomatoes and green chilies

1 (15-ounce) can black beans, rinsed and drained

¼ cup roughly chopped fresh cilantro

¼ cup water

8 organic corn tortillas

VEGETABLE SUBSTITUTION: SWEET POTATO

1. Preheat the oven to 400°F.

2. In a medium pan set over medium heat, sauté ¼ of the garlic in ½ tablespoon of olive oil for 1 to 2 minutes, or until fragrant.

3. Add the tomato sauce, vegetable broth, chipotle chiles, ½ teaspoon of chili powder, and ¼ teaspoon of cumin. Increase the heat to high and bring to a boil, and then reduce the heat to low. Simmer the sauce for 10 minutes.

4. In a large pot, heat the remaining ½ tablespoon of olive oil over medium heat. Stir in the remaining garlic, ½ teaspoon of chili powder, ¼ teaspoon cumin, jalapeño, and onion powder. Cook for 1 to 2 minutes, or until the garlic is fragrant.

5. Add the butternut squash noodles, diced tomatoes and green chilies, black beans, cilantro, and water. Stir to combine. Reduce the heat to medium-low and cover the pot. Cook for 20 minutes.

6. Cover the bottom of a large baking dish with a thin layer of enchilada sauce. Scoop ½ cup of the butternut squash mixture into the center of a corn tortilla and roll into an enchilada. Place it into the baking dish seam-side down. Repeat with the remaining tortillas and filling.

7. Cover the baking dish with aluminum foil and place it in the preheated oven. Bake for 8 minutes, or until the tortillas begin to brown.

COOKING TIP: *If you're short on time, you can purchase premade enchilada sauce and omit steps 2 through 4 and their accompanying ingredients.*

PER SERVING: CALORIES: 585; FAT: 7G; TOTAL CARBOHYDRATES: 108G; FIBER: 24G; PROTEIN: 29G

HOT-&-COLD
GRAIN
BOWL

This hearty dish is full of beautifully colored vegetables and makes it possible to put a nutritious meal on the table even on the busiest of days.

SERVES 2

- 2 cups cooked quinoa
- 2 cups packed baby spinach
- ½ **daikon radish**, spiralized into fettuccine noodles
- 1 **red bell pepper**, spiralized into fettuccine noodles
- 1 **carrot**, spiralized into fettuccine noodles
- 1 **jicama**, spiralized into fettuccine noodles
- ½ cup Tahini-Ginger Dressing (page 177), divided

VEGETABLE SUBSTITUTION: BEET, CUCUMBER, KOHLRABI, YELLOW BELL PEPPER, ZUCCHINI

1. Place 1 cup of quinoa into each of 2 bowls. Top each with 1 cup of spinach.

2. To each bowl, add half of the radish noodles, red bell pepper noodles, carrot noodles, and jicama noodles.

3. Drizzle each with ¼ cup of Tahini-Ginger Dressing and serve.

INGREDIENT TIP: *Try farro or brown rice in place of quinoa for a different twist on the grain component of this recipe. Farro is a bit softer and more tender, while brown rice has a nuttier, chewier texture than quinoa.*

PER SERVING: CALORIES: 356; FAT: 14G; TOTAL CARBOHYDRATES: 50G; FIBER: 14G; PROTEIN: 10G

BASIL-CELERIAC NOODLES

Celery as pasta? Yes, I'm serious! When celeriac is cooked, it becomes milder than it is raw—and this simple-to-prep creamy basil sauce is the perfect accompaniment.

SERVES 2

1 cup packed fresh basil leaves

1 cup full-fat coconut milk

¼ cup vegetable broth

6 garlic cloves, finely minced

Juice of ½ lemon

1 teaspoon Italian seasoning

Sea salt

Freshly ground black pepper

1 celeriac, spiralized into fettuccine noodles

VEGETABLE SUBSTITUTION: KOHLRABI, SUMMER SQUASH, ZUCCHINI

1. In a blender, combine the basil, coconut milk, vegetable broth, garlic, lemon juice, and Italian seasoning. Season with sea salt and pepper. Blend on medium until all the ingredients are combined. Transfer to a medium saucepan.

2. Place the saucepan over low heat and cook for 20 to 30 minutes, or until thickened.

3. Fill a large pot with water and bring to a boil over high heat. Carefully add the celeriac noodles. Cook for 3 minutes. Drain.

4. Immediately toss the noodles with the basil sauce and serve.

PER SERVING: CALORIES: 335; FAT: 26G; TOTAL CARBOHYDRATES: 22G; FIBER: 3G; PROTEIN: 6G

CREAMY GARLIC & HERB RUTABAGA NOODLES

I love a good, creamy sauce every once in a while. This rutabaga noodle dish is coated with a garlic and coconut cream–based sauce that complements the earthiness of this hearty root vegetable.

SERVES 2

1 (13.5-ounce) can full-fat coconut milk, refrigerated for 6 hours

2 tablespoons freshly squeezed lemon juice

½ teaspoon dried parsley

¼ teaspoon sea salt

¼ teaspoon freshly ground black pepper

¼ teaspoon onion powder

2 tablespoons extra-virgin olive oil, divided

1 medium shallot, peeled and chopped

3 garlic cloves, minced

1 rutabaga, spiralized into fettuccine noodles

VEGETABLE SUBSTITUTION: CELERIAC, KOHLRABI, SUMMER SQUASH, ZUCCHINI

1. Remove the coconut milk from the refrigerator and turn the can upside down. Open the can from the bottom.

2. Scoop out the solid cream and put it in a small bowl. Add the lemon juice, parsley, sea salt, pepper, and onion powder. Stir to combine.

3. In a medium skillet set over medium heat, heat 1 tablespoon of olive oil. Add the shallot and garlic to the pan. Sauté for about 2 minutes, or until fragrant. Stir in the coconut cream mixture. Cook for about 5 minutes, stirring, or until the sauce begins to boil. Reduce the heat to medium-low.

4. In a large pan set over medium heat, heat the remaining 1 tablespoon of olive oil. Add the rutabaga noodles. Sauté the rutabaga for 8 to 10 minutes, until tender.

5. Pour the sauce over the noodles and stir to coat before serving.

PREP TIP: *Rutabaga is one of the trickier vegetables to spiralize. If you find yourself having a hard time, cut the rutabaga in half and then spiralize it.*

PER SERVING: CALORIES: 645; FAT: 60G; TOTAL CARBOHYDRATES: 29G; FIBER: 9G; PROTEIN: 7G

CREAMY MUSHROOM & CARROT FETTUCCINE

One of my favorite things about spiralizing vegetables is how many colors a single dish might contain—and this one is no exception. From the bright orange of the carrots, to the lively green of the parsley, to the rich brown of the mushrooms, this dish looks and tastes vividly fresh.

SERVES 4

4 tablespoons extra-virgin olive oil, divided

4 garlic cloves, minced, divided

1 pound fresh mushrooms, diced

¼ teaspoon dried thyme

¼ teaspoon dried rosemary

¼ teaspoon fennel seeds

1 bay leaf, crushed

1 (13.5-ounce) can full-fat coconut milk

4 large carrots, spiralized into fettuccine noodles

Fresh parsley, for garnish

VEGETABLE SUBSTITUTION: BUTTERNUT SQUASH, ZUCCHINI

1. In a large pan set over medium-high heat, heat 2 tablespoons of olive oil. Add ¼ of the garlic. Sauté for 1 to 2 minutes, or until fragrant. Add the mushrooms and sauté for 5 to 10 minutes, or until the mushrooms begin to turn golden brown. Remove the cooked mushrooms from the pan and set aside.

2. To the pan, add the remaining 2 tablespoons of olive oil and the remaining garlic. Sauté for 1 to 2 minutes, or until fragrant. Add the thyme, rosemary, fennel seeds, and bay leaf.

3. Whisking constantly, slowly pour the coconut milk into the pan. Once combined, simmer the sauce for 3 to 4 minutes, or until it begins to thicken. Add the carrot noodles to the pan. Simmer for 5 minutes more.

4. Remove the pan from the heat. Add the cooked mushrooms and garnish with parsley before serving.

PER SERVING: CALORIES: 356; FAT: 32G; TOTAL CARBOHYDRATES: 15G; FIBER: 3G; PROTEIN: 6G

SQUASH
& ASPARAGUS RISOTTO

If you're pressed for time, this recipe might best be saved for another day. Making a successful risotto requires patience. This recipe doesn't contain any actual rice, but riced butternut squash noodles absorb broth just like arborio rice does in the traditional dish.

SERVES 4

1 **butternut squash**, spiralized into spaghetti noodles

1½ tablespoons extra-virgin olive oil

3 garlic cloves, minced

1 white onion, diced

4 asparagus stalks, roughly chopped

½ teaspoon ground nutmeg

Sea salt

Freshly ground black pepper

1 cup vegetable broth, divided

VEGETABLE SUBSTITUTION: SWEET POTATO

1. In a food processor, gently pulse the butternut squash noodles until a rice-like consistency forms.

2. In a large skillet set over medium heat, heat the olive oil. Add the garlic and onion. Sauté for 2 to 3 minutes, or until the garlic is fragrant and the onions are translucent. Add the butternut squash rice, asparagus, and nutmeg. Season with sea salt and pepper. Cook for 3 minutes, stirring constantly.

3. While stirring, slowly add ½ cup of vegetable broth. Cook, continuing to stir, allowing the broth to incorporate into the rice. Add ¼ cup of the remaining vegetable broth. Cook, stirring, while the liquid reduces and incorporates.

4. If the rice is not fully tender, add the remaining ¼ cup of vegetable broth. Cook, stirring, while the liquid reduces.

5. Serve immediately.

COOKING TIP: *Take care to add your liquid very slowly and stir constantly.*

PER SERVING: CALORIES: 105; FAT: 6G; TOTAL CARBOHYDRATES: 13G; FIBER: 2G; PROTEIN: 3G

VEGETABLE
SOUP

This vegetable soup is full of hearty fresh vegetables both appetizing and nutritious. The spiralized vegetable noodles not only replace traditional noodles without sacrificing flavor, but also seriously cut down on prep time. After all, you can spiralize a vegetable in less than 60 seconds. What are you waiting for?

SERVES 4

1 tablespoon butter or grass-fed butter

1 yellow onion, spiralized into spaghetti noodles

⅛ **butternut squash,** spiralized into spaghetti noodles

1 broccoli stem, spiralized into spaghetti noodles

2 carrots, spiralized into spaghetti noodles

1½ cups coarsely chopped mushrooms

3 cups vegetable broth

¾ teaspoon ground cumin

1 teaspoon dried thyme

2 teaspoons dried basil

Sea salt

Freshly ground black pepper

VEGETABLE SUBSTITUTION: CELERIAC, POTATO, SUMMER SQUASH, SWEET POTATO, TURNIP, ZUCCHINI

1. In a large pot set over medium heat, melt the butter. Add the onion noodles, butternut squash noodles, broccoli noodles, and carrot noodles. Stir in the mushrooms, vegetable broth, cumin, thyme, and basil. Season with sea salt and pepper.

2. Cover the pot. Reduce the heat to low. Cook for 1 hour.

PER SERVING: CALORIES: 109; FAT: 4G; TOTAL CARBOHYDRATES: 13G; FIBER: 3G; PROTEIN: 6G

SWEET POTATO & MUSHROOM SLIDERS

There's something about sliders and food in miniature form that gives off this "too cute to eat" vibe. These sweet potato sliders are adorable, but I guarantee you'll want to eat them. Immediately.

SERVES 4

- 1 **sweet potato**, spiralized into fettuccine noodles
- 1 **small red onion**, spiralized into fettuccine noodles
- 2 garlic cloves, minced
- ¼ cup whole-wheat flour or almond flour
- 1 egg
- ½ teaspoon ground cumin
- ¼ teaspoon ground coriander
- ¼ teaspoon chili powder
- 3 tablespoons coconut oil, divided
- 16 button mushrooms

VEGETABLE SUBSTITUTION:
BUTTERNUT SQUASH

1. Line a baking sheet with wax paper.

2. In a food processor, gently pulse the sweet potato noodles and onion noodles until a rice-like consistency forms. Transfer to a large bowl. Add the garlic, flour, egg, cumin, coriander, and chili powder. Stir to combine.

3. Using your hands, form 8 (1-inch) patties. Place them on the prepared sheet.

4. In a large skillet set over medium heat, heat 1 tablespoon of coconut oil. Carefully add the patties to the skillet. Fry for 3 minutes or until browned. Flip and fry for 3 minutes more, or until browned. Remove from the heat and set aside.

5. In another large skillet set over medium-low heat, heat the remaining 2 tablespoons of coconut oil. Add the mushrooms. Cook for 5 to 6 minutes, or until tender. Remove the mushrooms from the pan.

6. To create a slider, place 1 mushroom face-up on a platter. Top with 1 sweet potato patty and top with another mushroom. Repeat with the remaining mushrooms and patties.

7. Serve with your choice of dipping sauces.

PER SERVING: CALORIES: 178; FAT: 12G;
TOTAL CARBOHYDRATES: 15G; FIBER: 2G; PROTEIN: 5G

VEGAN
RAMEN
BOWL

This is not your average college-student's instant ramen—that dorm-room mainstay and poor substitute for the original steaming bowl of rich Japanese flavor. The variety of spiralized noodles in a tasty broth will have you kicking that foam cup to the curb.

SERVES 4

- **4 zucchini**, spiralized into spaghetti noodles
- **4 carrots**, spiralized into spaghetti noodles
- ¼ **red cabbage**, spiralized into spaghetti-like strands
- ½ **white onion**, spiralized into spaghetti noodles
- 6 cups water
- ½ white onion, diced
- 1 celery stalk, diced
- 1 garlic clove, finely chopped
- 2¼ teaspoons miso paste
- ½ teaspoon ground ginger

VEGETABLE SUBSTITUTION: SUMMER SQUASH

1. Put the zucchini noodles, carrot noodles, red cabbage noodles, and onion noodles on separate paper towel–lined plates to dry a bit.

2. In a large pot set over high heat, combine the water, onion, celery, garlic, miso paste, and ground ginger. Bring to a boil. Reduce the heat to low. Simmer for 1 hour.

3. Add the carrot noodles, cabbage noodles, and onion noodles to the pot. Increase the heat to high. Bring to a boil and cook for 3 minutes.

4. Evenly divide the zucchini noodles among 4 bowls. Ladle the hot broth and vegetable noodles over the zucchini noodles and serve.

INGREDIENT TIP: *This recipe doesn't include a gluten-free label because miso paste often contains traces of gluten. If you can, look for a gluten-free variety and use it in equal quantity to what's called for in the recipe.*

PER SERVING: CALORIES: 83; FAT: 1G; TOTAL CARBOHYDRATES: 18G; FIBER 5G; PROTEIN: 4G

WALNUT PESTO TURNIP NOODLES

The mellow sweetness of these lightly cooked turnip noodles combined with the nutty, salty nature of the pesto makes this unlikely pair a standout on the dinner table.

SERVES 2

1½ tablespoons extra-virgin olive oil
2 turnips, spiralized into spaghetti noodles
1 cup Walnut Pesto (page 179)

VEGETABLE SUBSTITUTION: CELERIAC, KOHLRABI, SUMMER SQUASH, ZUCCHINI

1. In a large skillet set over medium heat, heat the olive oil. Add the turnip noodles. Cook for 6 to 8 minutes, or until the noodles are tender.

2. Stir in the Walnut Pesto sauce, coating all the noodles evenly, and serve.

PER SERVING: CALORIES: 151; FAT: 15G; TOTAL CARBOHYDRATES: 5G; FIBER: 2G; PROTEIN: 2G

BUTTERNUT SQUASH & SPINACH BAKE

The word "casserole" evokes images of mysterious, hot, bubbling dishes served at family gatherings and potlucks. This recipe is technically a casserole but, thankfully, doesn't match the stereotype—I think you'll recognize (and enjoy) all the familiar yet fresh ingredients.

SERVES 6

Coconut oil, for greasing

1 (1- to 3-pound) butternut squash, spiralized into ribbon noodles

2 cups packed baby spinach

4 tablespoons extra-virgin olive oil

1 white onion, diced

1 garlic clove, minced

1 cup full-fat coconut milk

½ cup flax meal

2 eggs, whisked

1 teaspoon dried thyme

Sea salt

Freshly ground black pepper

VEGETABLE SUBSTITUTION: SWEET POTATO

1. Preheat the oven to 350°F, and then grease a large baking dish with coconut oil.

2. Bring a large pot of water to a boil over high heat. Add the squash noodles. Cook for 2 minutes. Add the spinach. Cook for 1 minute more. Drain and set the vegetables aside.

3. In a large pot set over medium-high heat, heat the olive oil. Add the onion and garlic. Sauté for about 2 minutes, or until fragrant.

4. Remove the pot from the heat. Stir in the squash noodles and spinach, coconut milk, flax meal, eggs, and thyme. Season with sea salt and pepper.

5. Transfer the mixture to the prepared dish and place it in the preheated oven. Bake for 45 minutes. Serve immediately.

SUBSTITUTION TIP: *To make this a vegan-friendly dish, substitute flax eggs. For each egg, combine 1 tablespoon of ground flax seed with 3 tablespoons of water. Stir well, and place in the fridge to set for 15 minutes.*

PER SERVING: CALORIES: 337; FAT: 28G; TOTAL CARBOHYDRATES: 23G; FIBER: 8G; PROTEIN: 8G

Apple & Carrot Coleslaw 112

Asian Broccoli Slaw 113

Carrot Noodles with Tahini-Ginger Dressing 115

Cucumber Rolls 116

Cucumber, Watermelon & Mint Salad 117

raw

Jicama Noodle Bowl 118

Raw Pasta Salad 119

Pickled Cucumbers, Carrots & Daikon Radish 120

Spring Rolls 122

Tomato & Avocado Pesto Pasta 123

APPLE & CARROT
COLESLAW

No gloppy mayo-drenched slaw here. This raw coleslaw has rocked my world. It's made completely from whole, clean ingredients and is packed with flavor. Not to mention, its multicolored noodles make your plate so darn pretty.

SERVES 4

- **1 head green cabbage**, spiralized into spaghetti-like strands
- **1 head red cabbage**, spiralized into spaghetti-like strands
- **2 carrots**, spiralized into spaghetti noodles
- **1 Granny Smith apple**, spiralized into spaghetti noodles
- 2 tablespoons Homemade Mayonnaise (page 174)
- 3 tablespoons extra-virgin olive oil
- 1 tablespoon apple cider vinegar
- Juice of 1 lemon
- Poppy seeds, for garnishing
- Sea salt
- Freshly ground black pepper

VEGETABLE SUBSTITUTION: CHAYOTE, PEAR, SUMMER SQUASH, ZUCCHINI

1. In a large bowl, combine the green cabbage noodles, red cabbage noodles, carrot noodles, and apple noodles.

2. In a small bowl, whisk together the Homemade Mayonnaise, olive oil, cider vinegar, and lemon juice.

3. Pour the mayonnaise mixture over the noodles and mix well.

4. Sprinkle with poppy seeds and season with sea salt and pepper.

5. Cover and refrigerate for at least 1 hour before serving.

PER SERVING: CALORIES: 247; FAT: 14G; TOTAL CARBOHYDRATES: 32G; FIBER: 11G; PROTEIN: 5G

ASIAN
BROCCOLI
SLAW

It's tempting to buy prepackaged coleslaw and broccoli slaw mix at the market because all the work is done for you—but it always seems something in the bag has begun to turn when you go to use it. This quick-to-prepare recipe combines two easy-to-spiralize veggies with a tasty dressing for a slaw that's fresh as can be and sure to delight your taste buds.

SERVES 4

FOR THE DRESSING

½ cup extra-virgin olive oil

½ cup apple cider vinegar

¼ cup raw honey

1 teaspoon sesame oil

½ teaspoon soy sauce or coconut aminos

FOR THE SLAW

1 **medium head red cabbage**, spiralized into spaghetti-like strands

2 **broccoli stems**, spiralized into spaghetti noodles

¼ cup chopped scallions

2 tablespoons slivered almonds

Sesame seeds, for garnish (optional)

VEGETABLE SUBSTITUTION: GREEN CABBAGE

1. In a medium bowl, whisk together the olive oil, cider vinegar, honey, sesame oil, and soy sauce.

2. With a pair of kitchen scissors, cut the cabbage noodles and broccoli noodles into 3-inch-long pieces. Transfer to a large bowl.

3. Add the scallions and almonds. With tongs, gently toss to combine the ingredients. Toss with the dressing and stir to combine.

4. Garnish with the sesame seeds (if using).

PER SERVING: CALORIES: 397; FAT: 28G; TOTAL CARBOHYDRATES: 37G; FIBER: 6G; PROTEIN: 5G

CARROT
NOODLES WITH
TAHINI-GINGER
DRESSING

One of my friends gets cold noodles with peanut sauce whenever she orders Chinese takeout. I created this version—carrot noodles coated with Tahini-Ginger Dressing—as a fresh and crunchy homage to her delivery cravings.

SERVES 2

4 large carrots, spiralized into spaghetti noodles

½ cup Tahini-Ginger Dressing (page 177)

¼ cup peanuts, coarsely chopped (optional)

1. In a large bowl, combine the carrot noodles and Tahini-Ginger Dressing. Toss to coat, ensuring the noodles are fully coated.

2. Top with chopped peanuts before serving (if using).

PER SERVING: CALORIES: 392; FAT: 31G; TOTAL CARBOHYDRATES: 23G; FIBER: 7G; PROTEIN: 9G

CUCUMBER
ROLLS

I went on a cruise in high school with my best friend and her family. Every afternoon we would head to the sushi bar for a variety of rolls to take to the deck to enjoy while soaking in the sun and sea breeze. At the time I wasn't a big fan of fish, so I asked the chef to make a vegetarian option. Those yummy veggie rolls inspired this recipe. For a grain-free sushi option, fill the spiralized cucumber noodles with crabmeat or fish.

SERVES 2

- ½ cup cashews, soaked in water for at least 4 hours and drained
- 1 tablespoon water
- 1 teaspoon sesame oil
- ½ teaspoon tahini
- ¼ teaspoon sea salt
- 2 garlic cloves, minced
- **2 cucumbers**, spiralized into ribbon noodles, cut into 6-inch pieces
- **1 carrot**, spiralized into spaghetti noodles, roughly cut into 2-inch pieces
- **1 zucchini**, spiralized into spaghetti noodles, roughly cut into 2-inch pieces
- **2 radishes**, spiralized into spaghetti noodles, roughly cut into 2-inch pieces

VEGETABLE SUBSTITUTION: CABBAGE

1. In a food processor, combine the drained cashews, water, sesame oil, tahini, sea salt, and garlic. Process until a paste forms. The paste should be mostly smooth with some visible texture remaining.

2. Place the cucumber noodles on a flat work surface. Spread the cashew paste over half the length of each cucumber noodle.

3. Lay the carrot noodles, zucchini noodles, and radish noodles on top of the cashew paste. They can stick off one side of the cucumber noodles, but should be even with the other side.

4. Working one at a time, starting at the end that is full of the vegetable noodles, roll each cucumber slice into a roll.

COOKING TIP: *If you prefer a "no frills" cashew paste, omit the sesame oil, tahini, sea salt, and garlic. You will still end up with a delicious cashew paste that provides great texture for this recipe.*

PER SERVING: CALORIES: 303; FAT: 19G; TOTAL CARBOHYDRATES: 39G; FIBER: 5G; PROTEIN: 9G

CUCUMBER,
WATERMELON &
MINT SALAD

Do you ever eat something that reminds you of a season? This salad means summer to me—with its bright colors and fresh ingredients, this refreshing, minty combination will cool you down at the end of a hot and humid day.

SERVES 4

- 2 cups watermelon, diced
- ½ **English cucumber**, spiralized into spaghetti noodles
- ½ **small red onion**, spiralized into spaghetti noodles
- 1 tablespoon minced fresh mint leaves
- 2 tablespoons balsamic vinegar
- 2 tablespoons extra-virgin olive oil
- Sea salt
- Freshly ground black pepper

1. In a large bowl, combine the watermelon, cucumber noodles, red onion noodles, and mint leaves.

2. In a small bowl, whisk together the balsamic vinegar and olive oil. Season with sea salt and pepper.

3. Pour the dressing over the salad and toss to coat.

SUBSTITUTION TIP: *If your local market doesn't stock English cucumbers, substitute regular cucumbers. Peel off some of the skin before spiralizing, as it isn't as thin as that on an English cucumber.*

PER SERVING: CALORIES: 94; FAT: 7G; TOTAL CARBOHYDRATES: 8G; FIBER: 1G; PROTEIN: 1G

JICAMA
NOODLE
BOWL

Jicama is a versatile root. It easily can find its way into salads, salsas, stir-fries, or simply into your hand as a snack on its own. In this bowl, bright white jicama noodles combine with a colorful collection of other vegetable noodles and are topped with a tangy dressing.

SERVES 4

2 jicamas, spiralized into spaghetti noodles

2 yellow bell peppers, spiralized into spaghetti noodles

½ red cabbage, spiralized into spaghetti-like strands

1 cup roughly chopped Italian kale, thoroughly washed

½ cup diced scallions

¼ cup Tahini-Ginger Dressing (page 177)

VEGETABLE SUBSTITUTION: ORANGE PEPPER, RED PEPPER

1. In a large bowl, combine the jicama noodles, yellow bell pepper noodles, red cabbage noodles, kale, scallions, and Tahini-Ginger Dressing.

2. Toss to coat the ingredients evenly.

INGREDIENT TIP: *Italian kale has several different names: Tuscan, lacinato, black, dinosaur . . . the list goes on. This type of kale has a flat leaf and is a much darker color than its curly leafed counterpart.*

PER SERVING: CALORIES: 212; FAT: 6G; TOTAL CARBOHYDRATES: 37G; FIBER: 19G; PROTEIN: 5G

RAW
PASTA
SALAD

I generally avoid pasta salads at parties because they have too many mysterious ingredients and too much mayonnaise. Now, I have nothing against mayonnaise—this recipe includes it in the dressing—but it's my own light, homemade version that doesn't overpower the freshness of the vegetable noodles.

SERVES 4

⅓ cup Homemade Mayonnaise (page 174)

3 tablespoons pure maple syrup

2 teaspoons white vinegar

1½ teaspoons extra-virgin olive oil

1½ teaspoons dried basil

1 teaspoon freshly ground black pepper

½ teaspoon dried dill

Sea salt

1 zucchini, spiralized into spaghetti noodles

2 carrots, spiralized into spaghetti noodles

1 broccoli stem, spiralized into spaghetti noodles

VEGETABLE SUBSTITUTION: CUCUMBER, DAIKON RADISH, RED BELL PEPPER

1. In a medium bowl, whisk together the Homemade Mayonnaise, maple syrup, white vinegar, olive oil, basil, pepper, and dill until fully combined. Season with sea salt.

2. In a large bowl, toss together the zucchini noodles, carrot noodles, and broccoli noodles to distribute evenly.

3. Pour the dressing over the noodles. Toss to combine.

COOKING TIP: *If you have time, allow the salad to sit, dressed, for 10 to 15 minutes before serving. This permits the flavors from the dressing to be absorbed by the noodles and soften them.*

PER SERVING: CALORIES: 160G; FAT: 9G; TOTAL CARBOHYDRATES: 21G; FIBER: 2G; PROTEIN: 2G

PICKLED CUCUMBERS, CARROTS & DAIKON RADISH

Pickling is having its moment—and I'm not just talking about the traditional cucumber. There are several methods of pickling, but this one is relatively quick and uncomplicated for getting that pickled taste using some of my favorite spiralized vegetables.

SERVES 4

- ½ cup red wine vinegar
- ½ cup water
- 2 tablespoons sea salt
- 1 tablespoon raw honey
- ½ teaspoon finely minced garlic
- **1 cucumber**, spiralized into spaghetti noodles
- **2 carrots**, spiralized into spaghetti noodles
- **1 daikon radish**, spiralized into spaghetti noodles

VEGETABLE SUBSTITUTION: BEET, BELL PEPPER, ONION, ZUCCHINI,

1. In a large bowl, whisk together the red wine vinegar, water, sea salt, honey, and garlic.

2. Add the cucumber noodles, carrot noodles, and daikon radish noodles. Make sure all the vegetables are completely submerged in the liquid.

3. Marinate for 1 hour, stirring the ingredients every 20 minutes.

4. Serve as a salad or on top of your favorite dish.

COOKING TIP: *The beauty of pickling vegetables is that you can customize the flavor profile easily. Try additional spices like dill, coriander, or black peppercorns for a different result in each batch. If you have leftovers, simply refrigerate them in a sealed container.*

PER SERVING: CALORIES: 57; FAT: 1G; TOTAL CARBOHYDRATES: 13G; FIBER: 2G; PROTEIN: 2G

SPRING
ROLLS

Unfortunately, when I think of spring rolls I think of the greasy, fried variety all too familiar from takeout joints. These rolls, containing 100 percent fresh, raw spiralized veggies—and not deep-fried—are light years away in terms of taste and nutrition. You might even want seconds.

SERVES 2

⅓ cup soy sauce or coconut aminos

2 tablespoons rice vinegar

1 tablespoon pure maple syrup

1 teaspoon sesame oil

½ teaspoon garlic powder

½ teaspoon ground ginger

6 rice paper wrappers

1 large carrot, spiralized into spaghetti noodles

½ head green cabbage, spiralized into spaghetti-like strands

½ daikon radish, spiralized into spaghetti noodles

VEGETABLE SUBSTITUTION: CUCUMBER, KOHLRABI, PEPPER

1. In a small bowl, whisk together the soy sauce, rice vinegar, maple syrup, sesame oil, garlic powder, and ground ginger.

2. Fill a pie plate or similar shallow dish with hot water.

3. Working one at a time, carefully dip each rice paper wrapper into the water. Remove after 5 seconds and place on a cutting board. Let the wrappers sit for 30 to 60 seconds to maximize the pliability of the paper.

4. Evenly divide the carrot noodles, cabbage noodles, and daikon radish noodles among the wrappers.

5. Working one at a time, starting at the bottom (side closest to you), roll the wrapper up completely to form a spring roll.

6. Serve immediately with purchased dipping sauce.

COOKING TIP: *Rice paper is extremely finicky, so don't be alarmed if you rip a sheet while trying to make these rolls. The secret is to wait until the paper has a sticky feel to it before rolling up the contents.*

PER SERVING: CALORIES: 293; FAT: 3G; TOTAL CARBOHYDRATES: 58G; FIBER: 8G; PROTEIN: 9G

TOMATO & AVOCADO
PESTO PASTA

As a food blogger, I have made a ton of friends who share my passion for good food. Each one, however, has a different food philosophy so things can get a bit tricky when we host dinner parties. This is my go-to recipe when the girls come over because I know that everyone eats veggies. The avocado pesto is creamy and luscious, but the zucchini noodles don't fill you up like traditional pasta. So there's still room for dessert.

SERVES 4

1 cup packed fresh basil leaves
½ cup extra-virgin olive oil
2 avocados, halved and pitted
½ cup walnuts
2 tablespoons freshly squeezed lemon juice
4 garlic cloves
2 zucchini, spiralized into spaghetti noodles
1 cup halved cherry tomatoes

VEGETABLE SUBSTITUTION: CARROT, JICAMA, KOHLRABI, SUMMER SQUASH, SWEET POTATO

1. In a food processor, process the basil, olive oil, avocados, walnuts, lemon juice, and garlic until smooth.

2. In a large bowl, combine the zucchini noodles and cherry tomatoes.

3. Add the avocado pesto. Toss together until the noodles are fully coated.

COOKING TIP: *For a smooth avocado sauce, mix your ingredients in a high-speed blender.*

PER SERVING: CALORIES: 549; FAT: 54G; TOTAL CARBOHYDRATES: 17G; FIBER: 10G; PROTEIN: 8G

fish & seafood

CUCUMBER
& CRAB
SALAD

My favorite sushi restaurant not only serves great sushi but also gorgeous side dishes that accompany the entrées. This restaurant pays as much attention to the supporting roles of the meal as they do to the star. One of my favorite sides inspired this flavorful salad—a lead performer here.

SERVES 4

- ¼ cup seasoned rice vinegar
- 1 teaspoon raw honey
- 1 teaspoon soy sauce or coconut aminos
- ½ teaspoon sesame oil
- 1 English cucumber, spiralized into spaghetti noodles, cut into 2-inch pieces
- ¼ cup fresh lump crabmeat, cooked and chilled
- 1 teaspoon sesame seeds

1. In a medium bowl, whisk together the rice vinegar, honey, soy sauce, and sesame oil. Add the cucumber noodles and toss to combine.

2. Evenly divide the cucumber noodles among 4 plates. Top each with about 1 tablespoon of crabmeat.

3. Sprinkle the sesame seeds over the salads and serve.

SERVING TIP: *It may be tempting to dress this salad early if you have guests coming and want to get a head start on meal prep. To keep the cucumber noodles crisp and flavorful, wait to dress the salad until right before serving.*

PER SERVING: CALORIES: 39; FAT: 1G; TOTAL CARBOHYDRATES: 5G; FIBER: 0G; PROTEIN: 2G

HONEY-GLAZED
SALMON
OVER TURNIP RICE

Cauliflower tends to be the go-to vegetable for Paleo-friendly rice dishes, but I find that turnips deliver a consistency much closer to the real thing. Fresh, ripe turnips are easy to spiralize and even simpler to cook. In this dish they soak up the juices from the honey-glazed salmon to produce a flavorful, decadent-tasting meal.

SERVES 4

1 tablespoon raw honey

2 teaspoons soy sauce or coconut aminos

1 teaspoon coconut oil

¼ teaspoon freshly ground black pepper

4 (6-ounce) wild salmon fillets

2 turnips, spiralized into spaghetti noodles

1½ teaspoons extra-virgin olive oil

1 garlic clove, minced

1 teaspoon minced fresh ginger

VEGETABLE SUBSTITUTION: BUTTERNUT SQUASH, CARROT, JICAMA, KOHLRABI, PARSNIP, SWEET POTATO

1. Preheat the oven to 375°F, and then line a baking sheet with aluminum foil.

2. In a small bowl, whisk together the honey, soy sauce, coconut oil, and pepper.

3. Place the salmon fillets onto the center of the prepared sheet. Drizzle the honey mixture over the salmon, coating all pieces evenly. Fold the foil over the salmon to create a sealed packet. Leave the salmon packet on the baking sheet and place it in the preheated oven. Bake for 15 minutes.

4. While the salmon is baking, place the turnip noodles into a food processor and gently pulse until a rice-like consistency forms.

5. Heat a skillet over medium heat. Add the olive oil, garlic, and ginger.

6. Add the turnip rice. Cover and cook for 5 minutes, stirring occasionally. Remove from the heat.

7. Serve the turnip rice topped with a salmon fillet.

PER SERVING: CALORIES: 351; FAT: 18G; TOTAL CARBOHYDRATES: 9G; FIBER: 1G; PROTEIN: 37G

LEMON-BUTTER SCALLOPS
OVER LINGUINE

I used to think preparing seafood was a tedious task, but this amazingly simple recipe can be on the table in 15 minutes or less. Zucchini spiralizes in less than 60 seconds and only takes 2 to 3 minutes to cook, creating both a speedy and a delightful base for these scrumptious scallops.

SERVES 4

- ¾ cup (1½ sticks) butter or grass-fed butter
- 15 garlic cloves, minced
- 2 pounds scallops
- 2 tablespoons freshly squeezed lemon juice
- Sea salt
- Freshly ground black pepper
- 1 tablespoon extra-virgin olive oil
- **2 zucchini**, spiralized into linguine noodles

VEGETABLE SUBSTITUTION: BROCCOLI STEM, BUTTERNUT SQUASH, CARROT, JICAMA, KOHLRABI, SUMMER SQUASH, SWEET POTATO

1. In a large skillet set over medium heat, melt the butter. Add the garlic and sauté for 1 minute, or until fragrant.

2. Carefully place the scallops in the butter. Cook for 4 minutes per side—the scallops will turn an opaque white. Transfer the scallops to a plate, and pour the lemon juice over them. Season with sea salt and pepper.

3. Set the skillet over medium heat, and add the olive oil. Add the zucchini noodles and cook for 2 to 3 minutes, tossing until cooked through.

4. Plate the zucchini noodles onto 4 plates. Top each with one-fourth of the scallops.

5. Pour the lemon sauce over and serve.

INGREDIENT TIP: *Zucchini noodles tend to release water when cooked, so avoid letting the noodles sit in sauce for long periods of time. Store any leftover noodles and sauce separately.*

PER SERVING: CALORIES: 569; FAT: 40G; TOTAL CARBOHYDRATES: 13G; FIBER: 1G; PROTEIN: 40G

TACOS
WITH
JICAMA
SLAW

Mexican cuisine is my all-time favorite, and my particular weakness is Mexican street food. When done right, it's vibrant and fresh, and a real pleasure. There is just something about that blend of fresh veggies and spices that really lights up your taste buds.

SERVES 4

FOR THE JICAMA SLAW

1 jicama, spiralized into spaghetti noodles, cut into 2-inch pieces

½ **small red cabbage**, spiralized into spaghetti-like strands, cut into 2-inch pieces

¼ cup chopped fresh cilantro

¼ cup freshly squeezed lime juice

¼ cup Homemade Mayonnaise (page 174)

1 jalapeño pepper, seeded and minced

FOR THE TACO FILLING

1 tablespoon extra-virgin olive oil

1 pound boneless skinless chicken breast, cut into ½-inch strips

2 teaspoons chili powder

1 teaspoon onion powder

¾ teaspoon garlic salt

1½ teaspoons paprika

1½ teaspoons ground cumin

½ cup water

8 organic corn tortillas

VEGETABLE SUBSTITUTION: CABBAGE, RADICCHIO, RADISH, RUTABAGA

1. In a large bowl, combine the jicama noodles, red cabbage noodles, cilantro, lime juice, mayonnaise, and jalapeño. Stir well to combine. Set aside.

2. In a large pan set over medium heat, heat the olive oil. Add the chicken strips. Cook for 2 to 3 minutes on each side, or until the meat is fully cooked.

3. Reduce the heat to low and add the chili powder, onion powder, garlic salt, paprika, cumin, and water. Stir well to combine, coating the chicken completely.

4. Build the tacos by placing chicken strips inside a corn tortilla and topping with jicama slaw.

SUBSTITUTION TIP: *This recipe calls for organic corn tortillas, but if you can't tolerate corn or just want to experiment with something new, fry some plantain tortillas from my Loaded Plantain Nachos (page 40) recipe.*

PER SERVING: CALORIES: 506; FAT: 19G; TOTAL CARBOHYDRATES: 47G; FIBER 14G; PROTEIN: 39G

HANGER STEAK
OVER ROASTED RADISHES

We're lucky to have an outdoor grill at our Boston apartment, but it does us no good when the temperature drops too low. In the deep of winter, I turn to this recipe because, even without a grill, you can still cook an excellent steak. This versatile steak is a winner when pan-fried, and pairs well with pretty much any roasted vegetable you choose.

SERVES 4

2 tablespoons paprika

2 teaspoons dried thyme

½ teaspoon dried oregano

½ teaspoon dried rosemary

Freshly ground black pepper

8 radishes, spiralized into spaghetti noodles

3 tablespoons extra-virgin olive oil

1 teaspoon sea salt

3 pounds hanger steak

6 garlic cloves, minced

VEGETABLE SUBSTITUTION: BROCCOLI STEM, CARROT, POTATO, RADISH, SWEET POTATO

1. Preheat the oven to 350°F, and then line a baking sheet with aluminum foil.

2. In a small bowl, combine the paprika, thyme, oregano, and rosemary, and season with pepper. Set aside.

3. In a medium bowl, toss together the radish noodles, olive oil, and sea salt. Spread them on the prepared sheet so they are distributed evenly. Place the sheet in the preheated oven and roast for 15 to 20 minutes, or until tender.

4. Place the hanger steak on a cutting board. Rub it all over with the minced garlic and then the paprika spice mixture.

5. Heat a large skillet over medium heat. Add the steak. Cook for 4 minutes. Turn it over and cook for 3 minutes more.

6. Remove the steak from the pan and let it sit for 10 minutes before slicing.

7. Plate the radish noodles onto 4 plates. Top each with one-fourth of the hanger steak slices.

INGREDIENT TIP: *Hanger steak is best sliced thin and against the grain.*

PER SERVING: CALORIES: 528; FAT: 23G; TOTAL CARBOHYDRATES: 4G; FIBER 2G; PROTEIN: 73G

TERIYAKI
CHICKEN &
BROCCOLI
NOODLES

I credit my mom with my love for Asian cooking. She has always been the adventurous one in the family, seeking out the best dim sum, and the hippest sushi restaurants in the city. Admittedly I don't cook Asian food often enough but, when I do, Chicken Teriyaki is usually on the menu. The tender chicken and crisp broccoli noodles blend together in a sweet and sticky teriyaki sauce that beats takeout every time in taste and nutrition—and you can get it on the table in a mere 15 minutes.

SERVES 2

- 1 tablespoon extra-virgin olive oil
- 1 pound boneless skinless chicken breast, diced into 1-inch cubes
- **2 broccoli stems**, spiralized into spaghetti noodles
- 1 cup Teriyaki Sauce (page 178)

VEGETABLE SUBSTITUTION: CARROT, CELERIAC, PARSNIP

1. In a large pan set over medium-high heat, heat the olive oil. Add the chicken. Cook for about 3 minutes per side, or until browned and fully cooked.

2. Gently add the broccoli noodles to the pan. Reduce the heat to medium.

3. Pour the teriyaki sauce over the chicken and noodles. Cook for 5 minutes, or until the sauce thickens.

PER SERVING: CALORIES: 681; FAT: 24G; TOTAL CARBOHYDRATES: 35G; FIBER: 5G; PROTEIN: 79G

ROSEMARY & LIME CHICKEN THIGHS WITH ROASTED CARROTS

Chicken thighs make an easy and inexpensive dinner, and adding a combination of lime, rosemary, and garlic transforms ordinary chicken into a delightfully fragrant and tasty meal. Served with a side of roasted carrot noodles, this dish can be ready in under an hour but tastes like you've been slaving all day in the kitchen.

SERVES 4

2 tablespoons extra-virgin olive oil
3 garlic cloves, minced
2 tablespoons mustard powder
1 tablespoon chopped fresh rosemary
1 teaspoon sea salt
1 teaspoon freshly ground black pepper
Juice of 2 limes
8 (3-ounce) bone-in skin-on chicken thighs
3 carrots, spiralized into spaghetti noodles
1 scallion, sliced

VEGETABLE SUBSTITUTION: BROCCOLI STEM, BUTTERNUT SQUASH, CELERIAC, DAIKON RADISH, PARSNIP, POTATO, RUTABAGA, SWEET POTATO

1. In a small bowl, combine the olive oil, garlic, mustard powder, rosemary, sea salt, pepper, and lime juice.

2. In a large resealable plastic bag, combine the chicken and olive oil marinade. Seal the bag and shake to coat the chicken. Refrigerate for 30 minutes.

3. Preheat the broiler.

4. Line a broiler pan with aluminum foil. Arrange the chicken thighs, skin-side up, and carrot noodles on the prepared pan. Insert a leave-in cooking thermometer into the thickest part of one thigh. Place the pan under the preheated broiler and broil for 5 to 10 minutes, or until the chicken turns golden brown.

5. Reduce the oven temperature to 375°F. Continue roasting until the thermometer reaches 165°F.

6. Remove the chicken and carrot noodles, garnish with the scallion, and serve.

PER SERVING: CALORIES: 534; FAT: 35G; TOTAL CARBOHYDRATES: 8G; FIBER: 3G; PROTEIN: 45G

TURKEY BURGER
WITH SWEET POTATO BUNS

My spiralizer teaches me something new every time I use it, but perhaps the biggest lesson of all is to think outside the box. That is exactly how this recipe came about. I love turkey burgers with sweet potato fries—always have. But there is something depressing about eating a burger with a knife and fork. So one night, while peeling potatoes, I thought I'd try slicing them into disks instead of spears and using them as a bun. Well, what was sitting next to the knife block? My spiralizer, of course. A light bulb went off and the rest is history.

SERVES 4

FOR THE BUNS

Cooking spray

2 sweet potatoes, spiralized into spaghetti noodles

Sea salt

Freshly ground black pepper

2 egg whites

1 tablespoon extra-virgin olive oil, plus additional as needed

FOR THE TURKEY BURGERS

1 pound ground turkey

1 teaspoon onion powder

1 teaspoon paprika

¼ teaspoon cayenne pepper

Sea salt

Freshly ground black pepper

VEGETABLE SUBSTITUTION: POTATO

1. Heat a large skillet over medium heat and coat it with cooking spray. Add the sweet potato noodles. Season with sea salt and pepper. Cook for about 10 minutes, tossing frequently to avoid burning the noodles. Once the noodles begin to brown, remove them from the heat. Transfer to a large bowl.

2. Add the egg whites. Mix together until the noodles are coated.

3. Fill each cup of an 8-cup muffin tin about one-fourth of the way with the noodle mixture. Cover each cup with a piece of parchment paper, pushing down so the noodles are compressed into a solid bun. Refrigerate for 15 minutes.

4. Reheat the skillet over medium heat. Add the olive oil. Once the skillet is hot, gently remove 1 bun from the muffin tin with a spatula and place it in the skillet. Cook each side for about 3 minutes, or until heated through. Repeat with the remaining buns, adding more oil as needed. Set the buns aside while you make the burgers.

5. In a large bowl, mix together the ground turkey, onion powder, paprika, and cayenne pepper. Season with sea salt and pepper. Form the mixture into 4 patties.

6. Place the same skillet the buns cooked in over medium heat. Add the turkey burgers. Cook for 5 minutes on each side, or until browned and cooked through.

7. Layer each burger between 2 potato buns. Serve with your favorite dipping sauce.

COOKING TIP: *Turkey burgers get a bad reputation for being dry and flavorless. Watch the patties closely so they don't dry out while cooking.*

PER SERVING: CALORIES: 445; FAT: 16G;
TOTAL CARBOHYDRATES: 42G; FIBER: 7G; PROTEIN: 37G

sweets

DAIRY FREE, GLUTEN FREE, PALEO, VEGAN

MINI SPIRAL
APPLE PIES

Nothing says fall quite like caramelized apples in a flaky crust. As summer winds down and the leaves begin to change, kick off the season with a fresh apple pie. When fragrant cinnamon floods the house, you'll know that fall is just around the corner.

SERVES 6

FOR THE CRUSTS

¾ cup tapioca flour

¾ cup coconut flour

¼ teaspoon sea salt

2 apples, chopped

¼ cup water

½ cup coconut oil, divided

6 tablespoons pure maple syrup

FOR THE FILLING

3 apples, spiralized into ribboned noodles

2 teaspoons vanilla extract

¾ teaspoon ground cinnamon

¼ teaspoon ground allspice

3 tablespoons pure maple syrup

FRUIT SUBSTITUTION: PEAR

1. *To make the crusts,* preheat the oven to 350°F.

2. In a large bowl, combine the tapioca flour, coconut flour, and sea salt. Set aside.

3. In a small microwave-safe bowl, microwave the chopped apples for 1 minute on high, or until softened. Add the water, 6 tablespoons of coconut oil, and the maple syrup to the apples. Use an immersion blender to blend until smooth. Add the apple mixture to the flour mixture. Mix together until a dough forms.

4. Divide the dough into sixths. Roll each portion between two sheets of parchment paper until it is ¼-inch thick.

5. Grease a 6 muffin tin with the remaining 2 tablespoons of coconut oil. Press 1 crust into each muffin tin and trim any excess from the top.

6. *To make the filling,* place a saucepan over medium-low heat. Add the apple noodles, vanilla, cinnamon, allspice, and maple syrup. Cook for 5 minutes, or until the apples soften.

7. Evenly divide the filling among the muffin tins. Place the tin in the preheated oven and bake for 15 to 20 minutes, or until golden brown.

PER SERVING: CALORIES: 472; FAT: 21G; TOTAL CARBOHYDRATES: 70G; FIBER: 11G; PROTEIN: 3G

GLUTEN FREE, PALEO, VEGETARIAN

CARAMELIZED
PEARS
WITH COCONUT
ICE CREAM

Ice cream has always been a favorite. I could eat it for breakfast, lunch, and dinner, and in both summer and winter. Here, I combine my simple yet decadent coconut ice cream with sweet caramelized pear ribbons for a luscious yet guilt-free dessert.

SERVES 2

1 (13½-ounce) can full-fat coconut milk

1 teaspoon vanilla extract

½ cup plus 2 tablespoons raw honey, divided

Juice of 1 lemon

2 pears, spiralized into ribbon noodles

1 tablespoon butter or grass-fed butter

FRUIT SUBSTITUTION: APPLE

1. In a blender, combine the coconut milk, vanilla, and ½ cup honey. Blend until smooth. Transfer the mixture to a freezer-safe bowl or loaf pan and freeze for 30 minutes.

2. Remove from the freezer and whisk vigorously.

3. Refreeze the mixture for 2 hours, whisking every 30 minutes (4 more times). Freeze overnight.

4. In the morning, combine the remaining 2 tablespoons of honey and the lemon juice in a small bowl. Add the pear ribbons and toss until well coated. Set aside.

5. Place a skillet over medium-high heat. Add the butter. Once the butter begins to melt, add the pear ribbons. Fry for 2 to 3 minutes on each side, or until golden brown.

6. Serve topped with a scoop of coconut ice cream.

INGREDIENT TIP: *Use this recipe to make all your favorite ice cream flavors. You can add ½ cup of frozen fruit, nut butter, or dark chocolate chips.*

PER SERVING: CALORIES: 616; FAT: 42G;
TOTAL CARBOHYDRATES: 60G; FIBER: 7G; PROTEIN: 4G

CHAYOTE
& BLUEBERRY CRUMBLE

Fruit crumbles and crisps are always a quick and crowd-pleasing dessert. You can make them with just about any fruit you have—here I used mild chayote to balance the flavor of bright, bold blueberries. If you prefer, substitute apples or pears.

SERVES 4

- 1¼ cups almond meal
- ¼ cup slivered almonds
- ¼ cup chopped walnuts
- ⅓ cup unsweetened shredded coconut
- 2 tablespoons ground cinnamon
- ½ teaspoon ground nutmeg
- ¼ teaspoon sea salt
- 4 tablespoons pure maple syrup
- 5 tablespoons coconut oil, melted
- 1 pint fresh blueberries, rinsed and dried
- **1 chayote**, spiralized into spaghetti noodles
- 2 tablespoons brown sugar, or coconut sugar

FRUIT SUBSTITUTION: APPLE, PEAR

1. Preheat the oven to 300°F.

2. In a large bowl, combine the almond meal, almonds, walnuts, coconut, cinnamon, nutmeg, and sea salt. Mix in the maple syrup and coconut oil until a crumble forms.

3. In an 8-inch-by-8-inch baking dish, layer the blueberries and chayote noodles. Spread the topping evenly over the top and sprinkle with the brown sugar.

4. Place the dish in the preheated oven and bake for 45 minutes, or until the topping begins to turn golden brown.

MAKE-AHEAD TIP: *To save time, make this recipe in the morning and keep it refrigerated until dinner. When you sit down to eat, pop it in the oven and it will be hot and crisp by the time you are ready for dessert.*

PER SERVING: CALORIES: 612; FAT: 45G; TOTAL CARBOHYDRATES: 50G; FIBER 12G; PROTEIN: 11G

FRIED APPLES
& CINNAMON

Every fall Julien and I pack up the car and head out of the city to go apple picking. It is one of my all-time favorite traditions that we have kept up ever since we first started dating. When we return home, our arms full of fresh apples, the first thing I do is heat up my cast iron skillet. Despite exhaustion from a long day in the orchard, I can't wait to dig into some fried-apple goodness. This recipe really brings out the apples' natural sweetness.

SERVES 2

1 tablespoon butter or grass-fed butter

2 apples, spiralized into ribbon noodles

1½ teaspoons ground cinnamon

¼ teaspoon ground nutmeg

FRUIT SUBSTITUTION: PEAR

1. Place a skillet over medium-high heat. Add the butter. Once the butter begins to melt, add the apple ribbons. Make sure they do not overlap.

2. Sprinkle with cinnamon and nutmeg.

3. Cover and cook for 6 to 7 minutes, or until soft.

PER SERVING: CALORIES: 151; FAT: 6G; TOTAL CARBOHYDRATES: 27G; FIBER: 5G; PROTEIN: 1G

SIMPLE
PEAR & ALMOND
TART

Pear and almond is a classic flavor combination. In late summer when fruit reaches its peak, let fresh pears be the star of your dessert. In this unfussy yet flavorful grain-free tart, the pears are roasted to bring out their natural sweet and succulent flavors, then topped with fragrant cinnamon and a drizzle of honey.

SERVES 8

- 1½ cups walnuts
- 1 teaspoon baking soda
- 1 teaspoon sea salt
- 1 teaspoon coconut oil
- **3 pears**, spiralized into fettuccine noodles
- Juice of 1 lemon
- 2 tablespoons raw honey
- 2 teaspoons ground cinnamon

FRUIT SUBSTITUTION: APPLE

1. Preheat the oven to 375°F.

2. In a food processor, gently pulse the walnuts until they become a fine flour texture. Add the baking soda, sea salt, and coconut oil. Pulse again until a dough forms.

3. In a tart pan, place the dough in the center and press it out until it covers the bottom and sides. It should be an even thickness all over. Place the pan in the preheated oven and bake for 15 minutes. Remove from the oven and cool.

4. Reduce the oven temperature to 350°F.

5. In a large bowl, combine the pear noodles, lemon juice, honey, and cinnamon. Toss until the pears are coated.

6. Arrange the pear noodles in the crust. Return to the oven and bake for another 15 minutes, or until golden brown.

PER SERVING: CALORIES: 214; FAT: 15G; TOTAL CARBOHYDRATES: 19G; FIBER: 4G; PROTEIN: 6G

NOT-YOUR-AVERAGE CARROT CAKE

I avoided carrot cake as a child—it *does* feature a vegetable, after all. This tasty dessert may be packed with carrots, fruits, nuts, and spices, but that's the key to its sinful goodness. My version is also dairy and grain-free, so go ahead and dig in. If you want to indulge even further, top with your favorite dairy-free frosting or whipped coconut cream.

SERVES 8

⅓ cup coconut oil, plus additional
    for greasing
4 carrots, spiralized into spaghetti noodles
2 apples, spiralized into spaghetti noodles
12 dates, pitted
¾ cup raisins
½ cup walnuts
4 eggs
½ cup full-fat coconut milk
1 teaspoon almond extract
½ cup whole-wheat flour or almond flour
1 teaspoon ground cinnamon
¼ teaspoon ground nutmeg
¼ teaspoon ground cardamom
¾ cup unsweetened shredded coconut
⅛ teaspoon sea salt
Juice of 1 orange

FRUIT/VEGETABLE SUBSTITUTION:
PEAR, ZUCCHINI

1. Preheat the oven to 350°F.

2. Line a springform pan with parchment paper. Grease lightly with coconut oil.

3. In a food processor, gently pulse the carrot noodles and apple noodles until a rice-like consistency forms. Remove from the processor and set aside.

4. In the same food processor, combine the dates, raisins, walnuts, eggs, coconut oil, coconut milk, and almond extract. Pulse until the ingredients are chopped and combined.

5. In a large bowl, combine the flour, cinnamon, nutmeg, cardamom, shredded coconut, and sea salt.

6. Add the carrot and apple rice, date mixture, and orange juice. Mix until well combined.

7. Spoon the mixture into the prepared pan and place it in the preheated oven. Bake for 1 hour, or until lightly brown and firm to the touch.

8. Remove from the oven and cool completely. Release from the springform pan.

PER SERVING: CALORIES: 414; FAT: 27G;
TOTAL CARBOHYDRATES: 41G; FIBER: 7G; PROTEIN: 8G

ZUCCHINI & OAT
COOKIES

Incorporating zucchini into dessert is a great way to sneak in a serving of veggies in an unexpected way. A cross between oat-meal raisin cookies and my famous zucchini bread, these soft and chewy cookies are sure to be a hit with kids and adults alike. I'll bet you can't eat just one!

YIELDS 12

1 small zucchini, spiralized into
  spaghetti noodles
1 cup gluten-free instant oats
¾ cup almond flour
1½ teaspoons baking powder
1 teaspoon ground cinnamon
⅛ teaspoon sea salt
2 tablespoons coconut oil, melted
1 egg
1 teaspoon vanilla extract
½ cup pure maple syrup

FRUIT/VEGETABLE SUBSTITUTION: APPLE, CARROT, PEAR

1. In a food processor, gently pulse the zucchini noodles until a rice-like consistency forms. Transfer to a cheesecloth or clean kitchen towel and squeeze to remove excess moisture.

2. In a large bowl, combine the oats, almond flour, baking powder, cinnamon, and sea salt. Set aside.

3. In a separate large bowl, whisk together the coconut oil, egg, and vanilla. Add the maple syrup and whisk until well combined.

4. Slowly add the oat mixture to the egg mixture, stirring to combine. Fold in the zucchini rice and then put the bowl in the refrigerator for 30 minutes.

5. Preheat the oven to 325°F, and line a baking sheet with parchment paper.

6. After it's cooled, divide the dough into 12 equal pieces. Roll each piece into a ball and place on the prepared sheet. Place the sheet in the preheated oven and bake for 12 to 15 minutes, or until brown.

7. Remove from the oven and cool on the baking sheet for 15 minutes.

SUBSTITUTION TIP: *If you can't find instant oats at your local market, place 1 cup of old-fashioned oats in a food processor and pulse 5 times.*

PER COOKIE: CALORIES: 87; FAT: 4G; TOTAL CARBOHYDRATES: 12G; FIBER: 1G; PROTEIN: 2G

ZUCCHINI
RIBBON
CRISP

Fruit crisps and crumbles are always a hit, but did you ever consider making dessert from vegetables? The mild flavor of zucchini makes this plentiful summer vegetable easy to incorporate into your favorite desserts. Serve with whipped coconut cream or coconut ice cream and take pride in the extra serving of vegetables with dessert.

SERVES 4

- 5 tablespoons melted coconut oil, plus additional for greasing
- **2 zucchini**, spiralized into fettuccine noodles
- 1 lemon
- ¼ cup almond meal
- ¼ cup chopped almonds
- ¼ cup chopped walnuts
- ⅓ cup unsweetened shredded coconut
- 2 tablespoons ground cinnamon
- ½ teaspoon ground nutmeg
- ¼ teaspoon sea salt
- 4 tablespoons pure maple syrup
- 1 tablespoon brown sugar or coconut sugar

FRUIT SUBSTITUTION: APPLE, PEAR

1. Preheat the oven to 300°F.

2. Lightly grease an 8-inch-by-8-inch glass baking dish with coconut oil. Layer the zucchini noodles in the prepared dish. Squeeze the lemon over the zucchini, removing any seeds.

3. In a medium bowl, combine the almond meal, almonds, walnuts, coconut, cinnamon, nutmeg, and sea salt. Slowly add the remaining 5 tablespoons of coconut oil and the maple syrup to the bowl, stirring continuously to mix thoroughly.

4. Spread the topping evenly over the zucchini. Lightly sprinkle the brown sugar on top.

5. Place the dish in the preheated oven and bake for 40 minutes, or until golden brown.

PREP TIP: *Although I usually opt to keep the skin on zucchini when spiralizing, I recommend peeling the zucchini for this recipe for optimal texture.*

PER SERVING: CALORIES: 414; FAT: 33G; TOTAL CARBOHYDRATES: 29G; FIBER: 7G; PROTEIN: 7G

kitchen staples

CLASSIC TOMATO MARINARA

DAIRY FREE, GLUTEN FREE, PALEO, VEGAN

Italians take their sauce very seriously. In fact, in our house, my boyfriend sets aside a full day to make a pot of his family's recipe "just right." Unfortunately, life is busy. So, over the past few years, we perfected his recipe to come up with this Classic Tomato Marinara—that doesn't take all day. This delectable marinara is bursting with the bright, juicy flavor of fresh tomatoes. *Buon appetito!*

MAKES 4 CUPS

8 ripe plum tomatoes, with an "X" cut into the bottom of each
¼ cup extra-virgin olive oil
1 small white onion, finely chopped
4 garlic cloves, minced
1 teaspoon sea salt
2 fresh basil leaves, slivered

1. Bring a large pot of water to a boil over high heat.

2. Fill a large bowl one-fourth full with cold water. Add ice to make the water very cold.

3. Carefully place the tomatoes into the boiling water. After 30 seconds, remove them and immediately transfer to the ice water.

4. Peel the skins and stems off the tomatoes and discard. Place the tomatoes on a cutting board. With a large sharp knife, roughly chop them into quarters.

5. Heat a large pot over medium heat. Add the olive oil, onion, garlic, and sea salt. Sauté for 1 to 2 minutes, or until fragrant. Add the chopped tomatoes and any juice on the cutting board to the pot. Cook for 4 to 5 minutes, or until the sauce starts to simmer. Reduce the heat to low. Simmer for at least 45 minutes, stirring occasionally, so the sauce doesn't stick.

6. Top with the basil before serving.

COOKING TIP: *Different people swear by different varieties of tomatoes for the best sauce. Whichever you choose, make sure the tomatoes are very ripe.*

PER SERVING (1 CUP): CALORIES: 176; FAT: 13G; TOTAL CARBOHYDRATES: 15G; FIBER: 3G; PROTEIN: 3G

CASHEW ALFREDO SAUCE

DAIRY FREE, GLUTEN FREE, PALEO, VEGAN

I have a rule at restaurants to order something I don't usually make at home. I found cream-based sauces incredibly intimidating, so I always served pasta at home with red sauce and opted for creamy Alfredo when dining out. It turns out, however, that this creamy sauce is not only extremely simple to make, but doesn't even require cream. This cashew-based Alfredo sauce provides a dairy-free alternative that tastes just like the real thing.

MAKES 1½ CUPS

1½ cups cashews, soaked in water
    overnight, drained
½ cup water
1 teaspoon onion powder
1½ teaspoons garlic powder
2 tablespoons extra-virgin olive oil
Sea salt
Freshly ground black pepper

1. In a food processor, combine the soaked cashews and water. Blend until smooth.

2. Add the onion powder, garlic powder, and olive oil. Season with sea salt and pepper. Blend until smooth.

COOKING TIP: *If you have trouble blending the cashews, add more water. However, keep in mind that more water will result in a thinner sauce, so don't add too much.*

PER SERVING (¼ CUP): CALORIES: 240; FAT: 21G; TOTAL CARBOHYDRATES: 12G; FIBER: 1G; PROTEIN: 5G

GUACAMOLE

DAIRY FREE, GLUTEN FREE, PALEO, VEGAN

I put guacamole on just about everything and, although it is one of my favorite condiments, it also makes a tasty and nutritious snack when served with plantain chips or veggie sticks.

MAKES 2 CUPS

¼ red onion, finely chopped
½ teaspoon sea salt
Juice of 1 lime
4 avocados, halved and pitted
1 jalapeño pepper, diced
½ tomato, chopped
Garlic salt
Freshly ground black pepper
Fresh cilantro, chopped, for garnish

1. In a large bowl, combine the onion and sea salt. Add the lime juice and let sit for about 10 minutes.

2. Score the avocado into small sections and scoop the flesh into the bowl. Stir in the jalapeño and tomato.

3. Season with garlic salt, pepper, and cilantro.

4. Use a potato masher to mix everything together until you reach the desired consistency.

COOKING TIP: *Adding the sea salt and lime juice to the onion first and letting it sit allows the acid to "precook" the onion. If you prefer raw onion, just add it in along with everything else.*

PER SERVING (2 TABLESPOONS): CALORIES: 104; FAT: 10G; TOTAL CARBOHYDRATES: 5G; FIBER: 4G; PROTEIN: 1G

HOMEMADE MAYONNAISE

DAIRY FREE, GLUTEN FREE, PALEO, VEGETARIAN

Homemade mayonnaise is incredibly easy to make, and provides a healthy alternative to store-bought versions filled with additives and preservatives. Impress your guests with fancy flavored mayonnaise, like chipotle or roasted garlic, by adding other herbs and spices. Experiment to see which seasonings you like best.

MAKES 1½ CUPS

> 2 eggs
> 1 cup extra-virgin olive oil
> Juice of 1 lemon
> Sea salt

1. In a blender, combine the eggs, olive oil, lemon juice, and sea salt.

2. Blend for about 20 seconds on medium to high, or until smooth.

3. Use immediately, or cover and refrigerate for up to 4 days.

PER SERVING (2 TABLESPOONS): CALORIES: 155; FAT: 18G; TOTAL CARBOHYDRATES: 1G; FIBER: 0G; PROTEIN: 1G

JALAPEÑO-LIME VINAIGRETTE

DAIRY FREE, GLUTEN FREE, PALEO, VEGAN

Salad dressing is an integral part of any good salad. This citrusy dressing is fresh, bright, and pleasantly spicy, making it a terrific option for kicking your everyday greens up a notch. It also works well as a marinade for chicken or beef.

MAKES 1¾ CUPS

> 1 cup freshly squeezed lime juice
> ½ cup extra-virgin olive oil
> 1 jalapeño pepper, seeded and minced
> 1½ teaspoons sea salt
> ¾ teaspoon freshly ground black pepper

In a medium bowl, whisk together the lime juice, olive oil, jalapeño, sea salt, and pepper.

COOKING TIP: *If you and your guests love spice, leave some of the jalapeño seeds in the pepper before mincing—but not too many or it will overpower whatever you are dressing. Keep in mind, the more seeds left in, the greater the kick. For a milder dish, simply remove all the seeds.*

PER SERVING (2 TABLESPOONS): CALORIES: 69; FAT: 7G; TOTAL CARBOHYDRATES: 2G; FIBER: 0G; PROTEIN: 1G

ORANGE-BASIL VINAIGRETTE

DAIRY FREE, GLUTEN FREE,
PALEO, VEGETARIAN

Making your own vinaigrette is, in fact, quite simple. Mix vinegar and oil, and season with sea salt, herbs, and spices. The bold flavors in this simple vinaigrette are sure to impress your guests—but you don't have to wait for company to enjoy it yourself.

MAKES ½ CUP

¼ cup extra-virgin olive oil
¼ cup freshly squeezed orange juice
1 tablespoon freshly squeezed lemon juice
1 tablespoon Dijon mustard
1 tablespoon rice vinegar
1 tablespoon raw honey
½ cup fresh basil leaves

In a mini food processor or blender, combine the olive oil, orange juice, lemon juice, Dijon mustard, rice vinegar, honey, and basil. Blend for 30 to 60 seconds, or until smooth.

INGREDIENT TIP: *If you think ½ cup of basil leaves will create an overpowering flavor, add only ¼ cup to the food processor and increase the amount until you reach your desired flavor combination.*

PER SERVING (2 TABLESPOONS): CALORIES: 69; FAT: 6G;
TOTAL CARBOHYDRATES: 3G; FIBER: 0G; PROTEIN: 1G

SALSA

DAIRY FREE, GLUTEN FREE, PALEO, VEGAN

Liven up your plate. It's no surprise that this salsa's bold flavors result from its fresh ingredients—chances are you'll never go back to store-bought salsa once you taste this homemade alternative.

MAKES 2 CUPS

3 tomatoes, diced
½ onion, chopped
1 jalapeño pepper, chopped
Juice of 1 lime
1 tablespoon extra-virgin olive oil
Fresh chopped cilantro, for garnish
Sea salt

1. In a large bowl, combine the tomatoes, onion, and jalapeño.

2. Stir in the lime juice and olive oil, stirring until the mixture has an even consistency.

3. Garnish the salsa with cilantro and season with sea salt.

PER SERVING (2 TABLESPOONS): CALORIES: 15; FAT: 1G;
TOTAL CARBOHYDRATES: 2G; FIBER: 1G; PROTEIN: 1G

SIMPLE APPLE VINAIGRETTE

DAIRY FREE, GLUTEN FREE, PALEO, VEGAN

When out to eat, I find olive oil and vinegar is the safest choice for a simple, clean salad dressing. However, when at home, I like to spice things up a bit. This vinaigrette is one of my favorites, and works just as well over a basic green salad or one more complex, such as Apple, Spinach, & Walnut Salad (page 80).

MAKES 1 CUP

- 1 cup apple juice
- 4 tablespoons apple cider vinegar
- 1 tablespoon pure maple syrup
- ¼ teaspoon sea salt
- ¼ teaspoon freshly ground black pepper
- ¼ cup extra-virgin olive oil

1. In a medium bowl, thoroughly whisk together the apple juice, cider vinegar, maple syrup, sea salt, and pepper.

2. Slowly add the olive oil, continuing to whisk until the dressing thickens.

PER SERVING (2 TABLESPOONS): CALORIES: 77; FAT: 6G; TOTAL CARBOHYDRATES: 5G; FIBER: 0G; PROTEIN: 0G

TAHINI-GINGER DRESSING

DAIRY FREE, GLUTEN FREE, PALEO, VEGAN

Tahini is one of those "behind the scenes" ingredients that appear in lots of Mediterranean dips, like hummus or baba ganoush. In this recipe, that sesame seed flavor combines with a kick of ginger to produce a versatile dressing compatible with salads and a variety of other dishes.

MAKES 1 CUP

- ¼ cup tahini
- ¼ cup extra-virgin olive oil
- ¼ cup water
- 2 tablespoons soy sauce or coconut aminos
- 1½ tablespoons freshly squeezed lemon juice
- 1½ teaspoons red wine vinegar
- 1½ teaspoons white wine vinegar
- 2 teaspoons minced fresh ginger
- 3 garlic cloves, minced
- Freshly ground black pepper

In a blender, combine the tahini, olive oil, water, soy sauce, lemon juice, red wine vinegar, white wine vinegar, ginger, and garlic. Season with pepper. Blend until smooth.

PER SERVING (2 TABLESPOONS): CALORIES: 105; FAT: 10G; TOTAL CARBOHYDRATES: 3G; FIBER: 1G; PROTEIN: 2G